# Dream.

# Plan.

# Travel.

Your Guide to Independent Travel on a Budget

## Cathleen Fulton

*Dream. Plan. Travel.*

All Rights Reserved

© 2019 Cathleen Fulton

ISBN: 978-0-9727759-9-1

Except for brief reviews, no part of this book may be reproduced in any form or by any means, electronic or mechanical, including photocopying, recording, or by any information storage and retrieval system, without the written permission of the author.

**On the cover:** Overlooking the Pinkuylluna Incan Granaries near Ollantaytambo, Peru. I chose this cover image for many reasons:
- It has a dreamy quality to it.
- It conveys travel to a foreign place.
- It makes me feel like the traveler is thinking, "Look at me! Look where I am! I cannot believe I am here." It is a "pinch myself" moment.
- I fee like the traveler is content and comfortable with her surroundings.
- I feel like she is in no hurry to leave.

...all things I want people to experience when traveling.

Layout and publishing by
*Capturing Memories*
www.CapturingMemories.com

*In memory of my mother,*

*Mary Jane Brunson Rhoades*

*Somehow, she knew I had the wanderlust before I did.*

# TABLE OF CONTENTS

**INTRODUCTION    5**
   Why This is Important to Me    5
   The Magic of Travel    6
   The Way I Travel    6
   Solo, Independent, Frugal, Slow, and Long-term Travel    7
   "You are Livin' My Dream!"    8

**HOW TO USE THIS BOOK    11**
   Additional Resources    11
   Using the QR Codes    12
   Signing in to CathleensOdyssey.com    12
   Using a Journal    12
   Some Things You Won't Find in This Book    13
   Affiliate Disclosure    13

**1 EXPLORING TRAVEL STYLES    15**
   "Don't You Get Lonely?"    15
   "Aren't You Afraid?" (Solo Travel)    16
   DIY Travel (Independent Travel)    20
   Slow Down, You Move Too Fast (Slow Travel)    25
   I'm Not Ready to Go Home  (Long Term Travel)    29
   What is Right for You?    31

**2 PLANNING IS HALF THE FUN!    33**
   Dream    33
   Plan    35

**3 ON THE MOVE    45**
   Stay Organized    45
   Checklist for Moving On    46
   At My Fingertips    48
   On Arrival    49
   Long-Haul Survival Guide    52

## 4 A Penny Saved... 55
16 Ways I Save Money When Traveling 56
Do Your Own Research 59
Always Know Where Your Money is Going 60
Saving on Lodging 62
Saving on Transportation 63

## 5 Food, Glorious Food 69
Frugal Food Strategies 69
Enjoying Local Cuisine 75
Cooking is a Way to Connect with Locals 77

## 6 Now I Lay Me Down to Sleep 79
Choosing where to stay 79
Hostels are not Just for 20-Somethings 83

## 7 Taking Care of Business 91
Your Personal Assistant at Home 92
Other "Business" Considerations 93
Working on The Road 95
Keeping in Touch 96

## 8 Stuff (or, What I Pack) 101
Think Small 102
Packing Strategies 103
My Portable "Office" 104
Useful Items I Don't Leave Behind 105

## 9 Off the Beaten Tourist Track 109
Finding the Nooks and Crannies 109
Low-Season Travel 111

## 10 Staying Well & Safe 117
Before You Leave Home 117
Practice Healthy Habits 118
Learn How to Make Water Safe To Drink 119
First Aid Kit 120
If You Get Sick 121
Safety 121
Insurance 124

## 11 MENTAL HEALTH   127
- Preventing Burnout   127
- Practicing Gratitude   129
- When Things go Wrong   133

## 12 ENHANCED TRAVEL   135
- Keep a Travel Journal   135
- Staying Creative   136
- Mindful Travel   137
- Thematic Travel   139

## APPENDIX   145
- Handbooks and How-Tos   145
- Favorite Places   145
- Favorite Blog Posts   147
- Cathleen's Odyssey Bookstore   149

## ACKNOWLEDGEMENTS   151

## ABOUT THE AUTHOR   153

---

### VIGNETTES
- Courage   17
- Perros Malos!   19
- The Women of Chucuito   26
- Cutting the Queue   53
- "But I've Gotta' Driver and That's a Start"   64
- The Hospitality of Strangers   82
- The Black Sheep Hostel   87
- Off-the-Beaten-Path Rewards   109
- The Wild Atlantic   112
- The Women of Patabamba   114
- Sick as a Dog in Malaysia   125
- Finding Gratitude in Dissapointment   130
- A Couple Near-Misses   132
- Hamish, the Traveling Scarf   142–143

# INTRODUCTION

**IN THIE INTRODUCTION**

- Why This is Important to Me
- The Magic of Travel
- The Way I Travel
- Solo, Independent, Frugal, Slow, and Long-term Travel
- "You are Livin' My Dream!"

This is a travel book, but I have a hard time categorizing it. It is not just a travelogue. It is also not just a how-to-travel guide. I envisioned a work that would show how I travel as well as inspire others to find the travel style and methods that work for them.

## WHY THIS IS IMPORTANT TO ME

As our world becomes more polarized (politically and culturally), fear of the unknown is easily used as a propaganda device to create more fear and keep us in our place (our village).

When we actually visit and experience cultures and people that are different from us, we learn that the world is really not such a dangerous place. People who seem different from us at first really are not. Almost everyone in the world wants security for their families, food in their tummies, a dry bed to sleep in at night, and friends and relatives that care about them. We all want to share our experiences, laugh together, learn from each other, express ourselves through our art, and watch our children grow into adults.

I began travelling because I loved seeing new places and experiencing first-hand how other people live. Over the years, however, I have developed a personal philosophy about travel: not just

◀ *What's behind that little gate? The bridge looks a little scary. A friend could tell me what is there, but I would never truly know what it feels like, or who I might meet until I cross the bridge...one step at a time...*
*Bridge near Calca, Peru*

about how educational it is, but about how it is a valuable tool for personal development and empowerment; about how it promotes understanding among people who may be very different; and about how it could be a way to achieve lasting peace.

I feel that traveling authentically and independently—engaging with locals and learning how our similarities outweigh our differences—is an important avenue to peace.

If even 50% of us placed ourselves outside our normal lives for even a few months, we would reach levels of understanding and compassion that would be astounding.

## THE MAGIC OF TRAVEL

The first day I landed in Peru in 2014, I was so scared, I did not want to leave my guesthouse. But I did, and step-by-step I pushed out the boundaries that were holding me back.

*One long-term trip abroad and you will never be the same person you were before.*

After I had traveled a while, I found my mind expanding—opening itself to possibilities and finding opportunities everywhere I looked. I became more creative—so much so, that I had a hard time turning the flood of ideas off. Gradually I began to notice coincidences happening every time I turned around. It was like I had taken a magic potion. I cannot explain it, of course, but I have not taken these occurrences for granted. As a result, I find them happening more and more often.

Travel, especially travel outside your comfort zone, empowers you to live to your fullest potential, even once you return home. One long-term trip abroad and you will never be the same person you were before.

## THE WAY I TRAVEL

The way I move around this planet has evolved as I learned what kind of travel suited me. I am not that interested in most tourism sites. I've seen a few castles and plenty of cathedrals. I have difficulties remembering details of history and art styles. Geo-political topics lose my interest after about ten minutes. But sometimes I hear about a site or museum that sounds interesting and I might spend a whole day there, only to be chased out as the doors close.

## Introduction

Some that come to mind are the New Lanark Heritage Site in Scotland; the Slavery Museum in Liverpool; the Speelklok Museum in Utrecht; the Haapsalu Lace Center in Estonia; the Famine Museum in Ireland; and the Titanic Museum in Belfast. Do you see the pattern? These are all places where you can immerse yourself in a specific theme.

But I am most passionate about visiting places where I can connect with people who share interests similar to mine. My first sojourn as a "woman of a certain age" in 2014 was to Peru, which I chose because I wanted to meet knitters and spinners in the country where most of our alpaca yarn comes from. I took a leap of faith and got a non-refundable round-trip ticket that would not bring me home for 3½ months. Before I knew it, I was hooked on solo, independent, and long-term travel.

### SOLO, INDEPENDENT, FRUGAL, SLOW, AND LONG-TERM TRAVEL

I travel:
- **solo:** alone—although I have befriended a LOT of people along the way
- **independently:** making almost all my own travel plans; not using the services of agencies, tour groups, or guides
- **frugally:** I try to find a balance among affordability, comfort, and experiences. It can be a fine line.
- **slowly:** staying in one place for one to three months, so I can become accustomed to the culture, make friends, work on creative projects, and explore the area.
- **long-term:** more than the few weeks to a month which is common for folks on holiday

I have chosen these travel styles because they fit my personality and my sense of independence. Each has its pros and cons. Some people might enjoy traveling solo and long-term, but they would prefer having someone else deal with the planning and booking hassles. Some get lonely when traveling solo, or they really enjoy having a partner with whom to share the experience. Still others love solo and independent travel, but not for long periods of time—either because they enjoy their homes, friends, and family, or because they just cannot afford to be gone from work for more than a few weeks.

### "You are Livin' My Dream!"

As I travel, the questions I most often receive have to do with one of my styles of travel:
- Aren't you afraid? Is it dangerous?
- Don't you get lonely?
- Don't you miss home/friends/family?
- How do you decide where to go next?
- Can I watch you when you are making your travel plans? (i.e. researching where to go, how to book, how to get there)
- How do you travel so cheaply?

And so many people respond, "You are livin' my dream."

I get the idea that many people I meet would like to do something like this, but something is holding them back. It is important to determine exactly what is holding *you* back. Can it be overcome? Sometimes not. Until 2010, I had a profoundly disabled daughter. Rachel required care 24/7 and did not travel well. It would have been impossible (or exceedingly difficult) to travel with her, and I would not have left her in the care of others. In 2010, Rachel passed away unexpectedly at the age of 28. About a year after her passing, I realized that, if I sold my house and downsized a great deal, I could *go somewhere*!

*We each need to determine what holds us back from achieving any of our dreams.*

The main obstacle until 2010, was unsurpassable—I could not leave Rachel. But after that, my obstacles were financial and attachment to the home I owned. And there were solutions for those issues.

We each need to determine what holds us back from achieving any of our dreams. Is it family, debt, career, or something else? And we have to decide what is most important to us. I have found that journaling about the problem can help to unlock possibilities that are stuck in my head. Discussing my dreams with supportive friends and family was also very helpful. I discovered that a cheering squad of friends is an effective tool to not only embark on a dream, but also to keep that dream alive as I lived it.

## Introduction

And now we get to the root of what this book is all about. I want to be the first person in your cheering squad. By showing you the nitty-gritty of how I travel the world, I hope to not only inspire you to embark on your dream journey, but also to keep you supported with practical information.

Keep dreaming...

*Cathy Fulton*

Cathy Fulton
Otavalo, Ecuador

> *I believe that traveling authentically—engaging with locals and learning how our similarities outweigh our differences—is an important avenue to peace.*

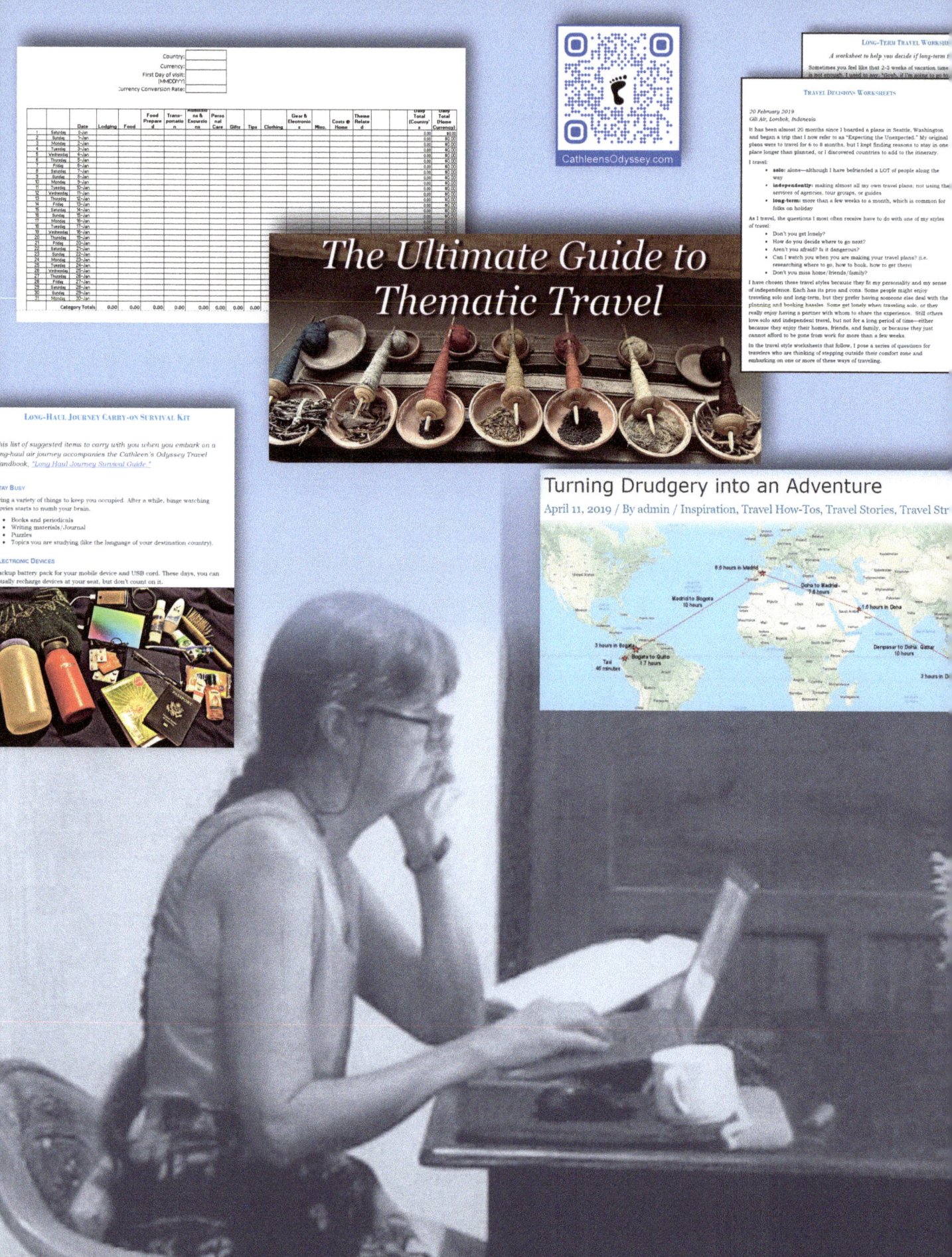

# How to Use This Book

**In this Chapter...**

- Additional Resources
- Using the QR Codes
- Signing in to CathleensOdyssey.com
- Using a Journal
- Some Things You Won't Find in This Book
- Affiliate Disclosure

Often during my travels, I meet people who ask me how I make plans, how I decide where to stay, how to travel, and how do I make the reservations. One person said, "Can I look over your shoulder the next time you are making plans?" This book is an opportunity for you to "look over my shoulder."

Whether you are a traveler, a wanna-be traveler, or an armchair traveler, I think you can find something useful in these pages.

Keep in mind, that I am sharing the styles and methods of travel that work for me. I am presenting them as "possibilities." Not everything you find here is for everyone. Pick and choose what appeals and works for you and leave the rest.

## Additional Resources

If I had included everything I wanted to in this book, it would have had far too many pages, and cost a lot more for you to purchase. By adding Internet links to related stories, worksheets, e-books, and products, I have enhanced the book's topics and provided avenues for you to explore the subjects that interest you more deeply. For example, in Chapter 1, under "DIY Travel," there is a link to an "Independent Travel Worksheet," a .pdf file you can download. It will help you decide for yourself if Independent Travel is for you. Some of the links take you to related blog posts, e-books, or products that I recommend.

I encourage you to explore these resources to get the most from your reading.

Dream. Plan. Travel.

## USING THE QR CODES

Most of the additional resources are accompanied by a QR code in the margin. If you have a QR code reader on a mobile device, you can scan the code and it will take you to the link that is referred to in the text. If you don't have a QR code reader, that link is also written out somewhere in a nearby paragraph, so you can also type it into your web browser manually.

For example, to the left is a QR code that will bring you to the home page of **CATHLEENSODYSSEY.COM**, my own website.

If you don't have a QR Code reader, you can find a free app to install in a mobile device by using an app store (like GooglePlay). Once installed, you use your device to scan the QR code and you will be taken to the referenced page.

## SIGNING IN TO CATHLEENSODYSSEY.COM

Sometimes when you follow a link, you will be asked to sign in to the Cathleen's Odyssey website with your email. You will be placed on my mailing list. I only send out emails to that list about every 2-4 weeks, so you won't be inundated with emails from me. You will mostly receive notices of new Travel Handbooks that I make available. These how-to guides will further enhance the content of this book. You can unsubscribe at any time by clicking the link at the bottom of any email you receive.

## USING A JOURNAL

You will see that I often suggest the use of a journal of some kind to daydream, record ideas, make plans, keep records, solve problems, and more. Decide for yourself the kind of journal you want to use. However, at the risk of sounding old-fashioned, I recommend that you use a hardcopy paper and pen for this kind of journaling. Over the years, I have discovered that something kind of magical occurs when you are writing with a pen that doesn't happen when writing on a computer—especially when trying to solve problems or make difficult decisions. I also find that "doodling" when brainstorming brings out ideas that I don't have when using the computer. You can also insert ephemera into a hardcopy journal, making it into a personal work of art that you and your family will cherish for many years.

## How to Use This Book

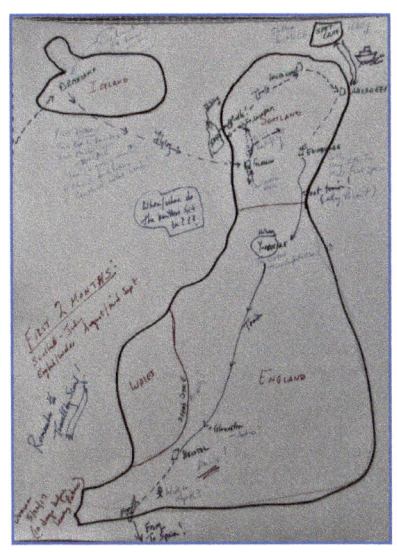

*You don't have to be an artist! Here is a daydream/planning map I drew when first considering my trip to Europe in 2017. Believe it or not, it is supposed to be a map of Iceland and the UK!*

Don't get me wrong, I also use my computer extensively to make plans, reservations, and contact people. I use a note-taking app, a word processor, a spreadsheet, and photo and video-editing software. I correspond via Skype, Facebook, email, and my blog. But I have several volumes of hand-written travel journals filled with poorly-drawn maps as well as lots of stuff taped and glued in the pages. I would not give them up for the world.

### SOME THINGS YOU WON'T FIND IN THIS BOOK

Each long-term traveler develops his own traveling lifestyle. You will see evidence of mine in the pages of this book. There are other ways to travel and I encourage you to discover what works for you, your passions, your personality, and your skills. Some travel topics I do not cover, but I believe are worth exploring are:
- Voluntourism
- Workaways, Wwoofing, or similar work-trade options
- Professional travel blogging
- Housesitting
- Couchsurfing
- Being an ex-pat

### AFFILIATE DISCLOSURE

In the interest of transparency, some of the links to products in this book are affiliate links, which means that if you choose to make a purchase, I will earn a small commission. The commission does not increase your cost. I recommend the products because they have been useful to me, not because of the small commission I receive if you decide to buy something. Please, only purchase products that will be useful for *your* traveling lifestyle.

# Chapter One

# Exploring Travel Styles

> **In this Chapter...**
> - "Don't You Get Lonely?"
> - "Aren't You Afraid?"
> - DIY Travel
> - Slow Down, You Move Too Fast
> - I'm Not Ready to Go Home
> - What is Right for You?

After many months of moving about, I figured out the method of travel that works for me. Of course, I would never expect anyone to travel the exact way that I do. Just because I am a person who enjoys doing things alone a great deal, that does not assume that you are the same way. For that reason, I have broken down my method of travel into several specific styles so that you can get some idea, before you hit the road, of which kind of travel will work for you.

## "Don't You Get Lonely?"

When people learn that I have been traveling for 20 months, mostly on my own, the two main questions I get are, "Are you afraid?" and "Do you get lonely?" I am rarely afraid, but I am careful where I go alone, and I do a lot of research about destinations so that I am somewhat acquainted with the location. In response to the second question, my answer is, "No." BUT that has a lot to do with my personality. Since I was quite young, I liked being alone and doing things on my own—

> One time my mom told me that when I was a wee thing, she could put me out in my backyard sandbox and I would play by myself for hours—a portent of what I would be like as an adult.

◀ *Helping the* ala kiyiz *carpet masters demonstrate how their traditional carpets are created. Jyrgalen, Kyrgyzstan*

making my own choices. Not everyone is like this and solo travel is not for everyone.

The main advantage of traveling alone is that you can decide where to go and how long to stay and you have all the say-so in your itinerary. For example, you never have this conversation:

"Do you want to go to Cibolo's for dinner or the pizza place?"
"It doesn't matter to me, where do you want to go?"
"I don't care...you decide."
"Okay...Let's get pizza."
"Oh, but they have fish at Cibolo's"

When traveling day after day, this sort of thing can get old.

*The main advantage of traveling alone is that you can decide where to go and how long to stay...*

When I travel alone, I find that I am more likely to make new friends, especially locals, and have more time to get to know them, than when I have a companion. I do sometimes go on short excursions with new acquaintances, and then we go our separate ways.

BUT, when you have a traveling companion, there are a lot more options of places to go and times to visit when you feel safe—especially if you are a woman. AND, you have someone to share spectacular experiences with, or to commiserate with when things go awry.

A good way to find out if you like solo travel is to try a short trip alone—maybe a week, or even a weekend—first. The same goes for traveling with someone with whom you have not traveled before—go on a little test journey together.

SO, solo travel is not for everyone. But if it is something you are considering, my Solo Travel Worksheet, may help you decide. You can download it at: **CathleensOdyssey.com/dpt-downloads**

## "Aren't You Afraid?"

This is probably the question I hear most frequently when people, especially women, learn that I am traveling alone. "I could never do that," they say almost enviously.

Yes, sometimes I am afraid when traveling. But no more often than when I am at home. Experience helps. Sometimes you just need to step out and meet your fears head-on. The next time you face a similar experience, the fear will have lessened.

Exploring Travel Styles

I am rarely truly afraid anymore. I DO take some precautions to preempt the fear or danger:
- I ask locals I trust if an area is safe to walk in.
- I pay attention to my surroundings when I use ATMs or am putting cash away.
- I try to stay aware of my surroundings. If the street gets crowded, I make sure my valuables are secure.
- I just don't go to areas where I think I might get hassled or that are notorious for danger—like the parts of Columbia where drug-lords still rule. (Although much of Columbia is now safe for travelers.)

> *Courage*
>
> *It was January 2014 and I was on my way to Peru--alone. I was scared.*
>
> *As the plane descended in Lima, the airline attendant announced, "Ladies and gentlemen, we are approaching the Jorge Chávez International Airport…," and everything inside me willed the plane to turn around and head back to Houston—to familiarity.*
>
> *What the hell was I doing? And it was almost midnight, for gosh sakes! Afraid of going outside at that hour, I spent the night in the airport. Then, I took a 16-hour bus ride to my first stop, Arequipa. I was exhausted, but more than that I was frozen with fear. I could not make myself leave the safety of my guesthouse. Eventually hunger overcame fear and I stepped outside. You can read about that at* CATHLEENSHANDS.COM/SHIP-IN-THE-HARBOR.
>
> *Making a long story short, two weeks later I was comfortable enough with my environment that I made an excursion alone to Puno and Chucuito to enjoy the Festival of Candelaria. I did the research and made all the plans on my own. I had become confident and overcame my fear in two short weeks!*
>
> *Yes, I was afraid. But of what? And in this question lies the solution to the dilemma. Fear is almost always in your head. I say it is usually an illusion. After all, how many people who ask me, "Aren't you afraid?" get into their cars every day and drive down the local expressway? Think about that for a second.*

"A Ship in the Harbor is Safe" Blog

- I use my US State Department's STEP program to notify me of possible dangerous activities going on in countries where I am traveling. More about that in Chapter 10.
- I ask myself, "What, specifically, are you afraid might happen, and what would you do about it?" It may sound ridiculous but fanaticizing how I would heroically protect myself calms me. I guess it makes me feel more prepared.
- Journaling in a free-flowing style about what I am afraid of, why am I afraid, and what I can do about it, can be helpful.

I do sometimes worry about things that can go wrong. Like missing a flight or finding myself without a place to sleep late at night (that DID happen to me once—when I was NOT worried that it might happen, interestingly enough! Read the story on page 132.)

*I sometimes half-jokingly tell myself, "Go ahead and worry a lot about that, then it won't happen."*

Here are some things I do to mitigate worrying:
- It sounds somewhat counter-intuitive, but it seems to me that the things I worry about the most never come to pass. So, I sometimes half-jokingly tell myself, "Go ahead and worry a lot about that, then it won't happen."
- I ask myself, "What is the worst that can happen?" Then I begin to come up with ideas for mitigating "the worst."

> *This happened in Indonesia. I had to take a boat from Gili Air to Denpasar to catch a series of four flights to Ecuador. I had allowed plenty of time between the boat arriving in Denpassar and the flight leaving. But, right off the bat, the boat was seriously late. Instead of panicking or blaming the boat company, I started thinking about how I would handle things if I missed my first flight. I envisioned myself calling my travel insurance company—that is just what I had been paying premiums for the past two years. Because I had a contingency plan, I stayed calm. (I did make my flight, by the way.)*

Here is the kind of fear I do have: I can be a reticent traveler—not a good trait for a solo traveler, I know. And it means that I might not ask for directions before I have walked a mile out of

> ### *Perros Malos!*
>
> *One day, riding in a* collectivo *(small local bus) in Peru's Sacred Valley, the woman next to me asked if I was* solita, *alone. "Tienes miedo?" she asked (Aren't you afraid?) I responded, "Solamente de perros malos!" (Only of bad dogs!). We laughed... but later that very day, alone on a trail, I encountered two large dogs protecting some sheep—with no person in sight. I realized they were just doing their job and if they were well-trained they would stay in the pasture. But I walked way around the field anyway. The dogs did not come after me. But my heart pounded for the next 15 minutes as I scoured the trail ahead for more of the beasts.*
>
> *After living in Peru, where street dogs run rampant, I am not as afraid of dogs as I used to be. I have learned how to read their body language. City street dogs are rarely dangerous—at least not during the day. When hiking in the countryside, I usually have my trekking poles. Dogs hate sticks, and I can wave the poles behind me when they are barking and growling at my ankles. I only need to stoop down and pick up a rock, and almost any dog in the world will shy away. If owners, or even other people, are around there is less to be afraid of.*
>
> *Again, experience has taught me to observe how rational my fear is, and to take precautions.*

my way. Or, I miss out on an incredible photograph because I am too shy to ask for permission. Or, (and this really happened!) I don't pull out my drop spindle to show a group of women who are spinning that I share a special skill.

My reticence does not make sense at all. Rare is the person who does not want to help with directions; most people are flattered to have their photograph taken; and every time I have pulled out my spindle, smiles broke out all around. "Sabes!" said one surprised woman in Chucuito, Peru, "You know how!"

*Rare is the person who does not want to help...*

But I am so afraid of being the "ugly American" or appearing foolish, that I tend to over-hesitate. Not a good trait for an independent traveler, I know. But I am working on it.

"Courage" Blog

If you want some inspiration, read my blog post, "Courage?" about how afraid I was to get on a bus in Arequipa.
CATHLEENSODYSSEY.COM/courage-blog

All this being said, I AM traveling as an "older" woman. It is rare that I encounter men who hassle me. If I were even 30 years younger, I would certainly have—probably justified—concerns about that, and take more precautions—like avoiding "partying" where large amounts of alcohol are consumed; not walking alone at night; saying that I am waiting for my husband; etc. But I might take these precautions in an American city as well.

*Our fears are often misplaced and mostly an illusion.*

Yes, bad things do sometimes happen to good people. But when people ask me, "Aren't you afraid?", I want to answer with another question, "How many times last week did you get in your car, fasten your seat belt, and proceed to drive down a freeway?"

Our fears are often misplaced and mostly an illusion.

> From my journal on my second day in Peru, 2014:
>
> *I know it seems crazy, but upon leaving the restaurant, I felt soooo good, and proud of myself for accomplishing such a simple task as deciding on a restaurant and ordering a meal. I walked down the street almost in tears at the prospect that I was really going to enjoy being in Peru! It is amazing what a decent meal can do for your soul.*

## DIY Travel

What does "independent travel" mean? It can vary from traveler to traveler. But most independent travelers:
- like to choose their destinations and itineraries based on their own interests.
- like to do all or most of their own travel research.
- only hire guides or go on guided excursions occasionally.
- travel alone or with a limited number of like-minded people.
- engage with locals, which often means staying in one location longer than most guided tours allow for.
- usually like to travel "off the beaten track."

*Engaging with locals….Spinning and knitting with the local Scottish ladies in front of the Scottish Parliament on International Women's Day, 2018.*

- enjoy "living locally," using public transportation, and local stores, markets, and cafés.
- are less interested in site-seeing and more interested in getting to know the people and culture.

The main thing that independent travelers don't do is join a packaged tour. Here are some of the advantages of those kinds of excursions.

- You don't have to worry about lodging or transportation; all reservations are made for you.
- A (hopefully knowledgeable) guide escorts you everywhere, and answers questions, solves problems, and makes suggestions.
- Many of your meals are included, meaning you don't have to search for the best places to eat.
- Special meals, workshops demonstrations, or performances are arranged for you with local teachers, artisans, and performers.
- Your guide will take you through the various attractions and point out the most interesting things.

- They are usually very secure—alleviating many fears new travelers have.

If you have never traveled to a region where the culture is vastly different from yours, if you are a new traveler, or if you are truly afraid of going abroad without help, a guided excursion could be a perfect fit for your first trip. But you might schedule a few days (or more) after the tour ends to remain in the country and try some independent traveling. By that time, you will be more comfortable in your new surroundings. It will be easier for you to visit places the tour did not include, return to a location that was on the tour and explore it more deeply, or meet some locals who share similar interests.

> ...schedule a few days after the tour ends to...try some independent traveling.

From the beginning, I have stayed away from these kinds of tours, mainly because they tend to be so expensive. They usually provide lodging and meals that I consider expensive. They include (sometimes hefty) admissions to some sites that I have no interest in. There are several middle-men who each get a cut of your fare.

There are other disadvantages:

- You are herded from place to place on a specific schedule. "Be back on the bus by 2:00," is the guide's mantra.

*I could have explored this northern coast of Northern Ireland all day, but alas, I had taken a guided excursion up from Belfast and we "had to be back on the bus in an hour."*

- You only stay two to three days in each location (often much less)—you do not get a chance to absorb the place before you have to move on.
- They tend to concentrate on the larger cities with the most tourist sights and things to do.
- If you are not enjoying some aspect of the trip, you are stuck waiting for the group.
- If you discover something that is especially interesting to you, you cannot linger to explore it for as long as you wish.
- If you have a special connection with a local, you cannot linger for another hour—or few days—getting to know them.
- If you get tired or sick, you can't take a day off without missing a part of the tour.
- They are just so sterile—you never get your hands dirty (metaphorically speaking).

"What about thematic tours?" you ask? Thematic tours do focus on a specific topic, like cooking, fishing, photography. My weakness would be any tours that focus on the fiber arts.

The nice thing about these tours is that the agency and guides do everything for you—transportation, lodging, food, tours and excursions. They organize special workshops and events for your group. You get to travel with other people who share your special interest.

A few times, I have been tempted to join such a tour—until I:
1. noticed that a great deal of time, the agenda had you spending up to a day moving from one place to another;
2. noticed that it included visiting sights that are not related to the theme and in which I have no interest;
3. realized a "12-Day tour," for example, includes the first and last days in which you are transferred from/to the airport and fed a meal (In other words, it is really only ten full days of activity.);
4. looked at the price.

Speaking of price: One twelve-day thematic fiber tour to Peru has a price tag of over $3800. (Remember, that means only ten full days.) That is a daily cost of over $300 which does not cover airfare or transfer to the first hotel. Looking more closely at the

Dream. Plan. Travel.

tour brochure I saw that only about a total of 30 hours are spent exploring the fiber arts—the rest of the time is spent visiting the typical tourist sights.

*I could eat in establishments so "local" that all heads turned in my direction as I walked in.*

In contrast, my 3½-month trip to Peru cost me $4,320 (not including round-trip airfare to Lima). That is less than $40 per day. I could choose where and when I wanted to go and change plans on a whim.

I made lasting friendships with many people on that trip. I was invited to parties; I could wander from village to village on a whim. I could eat in establishments so "local" that all heads turned in my direction as I walked in; when I found a place I enjoyed eating, I could return time and again becoming friends with the servers who greeted me warmly as I entered. If I felt a special attraction to a village, I could stay a month—or three. With a little guest kitchen, I could shop at the market like a local and learn from vendors how to prepare their food. If I wanted to, I could take

*On this gorgeous downhill walk from Chinchero to the Urabamba River, I did not meet one tourist, and yet it is in the heart of the very touristy Sacred Valley in Peru.*

days off from traveling pursuits to follow a creative urge—writing or knitting. Or I could spend hours with local women in the town plaza—all of us spinning or knitting together while they sold their wares to visitors.

Sound idyllic? Well, there are some downsides. I have to make almost all my own travel arrangements, sometimes spending hours on the computer looking at train, bus, or flight schedules, and deciding on which is the best lodging choice. On occasion the whole process would fall apart because a festival might be taking place at my destination and there would be no place to sleep, or the visa application was too complicated or expensive to obtain.

Without a guide, I quite frequently run into language problems or I get lost.

So now you have heard all the pros and cons I can think of regarding independent versus escorted travel. If you are considering traveling independently, download my "Independent Travel Worksheet" to help you decide if it is for you.

CathleensOdyssey.com/dpt-downloads

And, be sure to read Chapter 2 to learn how to become an experienced independent traveler.

## Slow Down, You Move Too Fast

Slow travel (staying in one place for at least several weeks) and long-term travel (traveling for longer than a month) usually go hand in hand. But it is possible to go to one location and stay for

> *Tourists don't know where they have been;*
> *Travelers don't know where they are going.*
> —*Paul Theroux*

Dream. Plan. Travel.

> **The Women of Chucuito**
>
> *My first experience with slow traveling was in Peru, when I decided to spend a month in the village of Chucuito near Puno on the shore of Lake Titicaca. I found an inexpensive guesthouse that gave me a special rate for staying a month. I was well off the beaten track. I had discovered it because I learned that the women in the area are famous for knitting finger puppets. These little treasures are exported all over the world to be sold in toy stores and gift shops. In Chucuito, the knitters and spinners gather on the square on Sundays to sell their wares, and that is where I met Yeni, Yovana, and Victoria, who I sat with several Sundays spinning, knitting, telling stories, and asking about families.*
>
> *You can read more about these women as well as Graciela, who sold raw alpaca fiber in the nearby village of Acora in my blog post, "Translating Tom Sawyer" here:*
> **CATHLEENSODYSSEY.COM/tom-sawyer**

"Translating Tom Sawyer" Blog

a month and return home (slow travel but not really long-term). And it is also possible to travel for a year, changing venues every few days (long-term travel, but not very slow). So, in this book, I am treating them separately.

Slow travel is a good style for those who want to take the time to pursue artistic projects or do research, especially with a theme based on where they are traveling. (See "Staying Creative" and "Thematic Traveling" in Chapter 12.) It also gives you the opportunity to immerse yourself in a new language, taking classes part time and then practicing in real life the rest of the day.

Slow travel affords you the time to explore the area—the food, hiking opportunities, and small out-of-the-way stores and cafés. It also gives you time to learn from locals about the places tourists rarely see.

Slow travel can also be therapeutic. I stayed three weeks in Alijo, Portugal as a sort of retreat after walking the Camino de Santiago. Some people might use the time to just relax, unwind and decompress after a stressful life event.

*A surprising aspect of slow-travel: You can only eat so much every day. The longer you stay, the more opportunities you have to try a wide range of regional food, or to return to a favorite restaurant, or to learn how to prepare these new foods. These were just a few of the dishes I was able to sample during my six weeks in Kyrgyzstan.*

Some people ask me, "Don't you get bored?" The answer is, "I don't." I think that if you are the kind of person who often gets bored at home, you will also become bored when traveling slowly. The key to warding off boredom, at home or otherwise, is to always have a variety of interesting things to do. Here are some of the things that keep me occupied, both at home and while traveling:

- Writing—I write for many different purposes: in my journal, blog posts, essays, books, and notes and texts to friends. I enjoy the creativity of writing and illustrating blog posts as well as making "mini-posts" on my Facebook page. (There's more about this in "Keeping in Touch" in Chapter 7.)
- Fiber Arts—I bring with me tools and a few supplies for

*I made this hat in the depths of winter in Ireland's Aran Islands, sometimes enjoying a half-pint of Guinness in the nearby pub. These islands are famous for this cable style of knitting.*

knitting and spinning. Since I look for knitters and spinners wherever I go, I gather quite a bit of yarn and spinning fiber to experiment with.

This could be applied to any special interest. Are you a musician? Bring instruments or purchase some in the places you visit. When on your own, try out new music styles from the country you are living in. (There's more on "Staying Creative" and "Thematic Travel" in Chapter 12.)

- Reading—I keep different types of e-books and audio books downloaded onto my tablet so I always have something to read.
- Planning my next adventures—I enjoy the puzzle of creating itineraries and researching places to visit. (There's more about this in Chapter 2.)

Routines are important for some people who are slow travelers. When I am staying for longer than a few days in one place, I find myself settling into a routine, just as if I were at home, waking at about the same time, getting breakfast usually in the same way, going for an hour long walk early in the morning, spending a few hours working on a project, eating a late lunch, etc. Of course, there are breaks in the daily routine for day hikes and other excursions, visiting a local site, or meeting friends.

Slow travel means traveling as a lifestyle. There is no one right way to go about it...just as there is no right lifestyle if you stayed at home in your community. You don't have to take advantage of every opportunity thinking you might never have the chance again. You might not, but you can never in one lifetime take advantage of every opportunity that comes your way—especially not in our modern world.

In the meantime, enjoy the little things...like buying a pastry from a street vendor and chatting with him about the ingredients; or just walking through the crowded streets or empty woodlands and allowing a "pinch myself"* feeling to overwhelm you. Every once in a while, you should exclaim out loud, "Look where I am! Look what I am doing!"

> *Slow travel means traveling as a lifestyle. There is no one right way to go about it.*

## I'm Not Ready to Go Home

Maybe you feel that the two-to-three weeks of vacation time you get every year is just not enough. I used to say, "Gosh, if I'm going to go to the trouble and expense to travel that far, I want to stay a while!"

Of course, the cost is the first thing that comes to mind for most of us. When I first went to Peru for four months, I was able to work for my clients on-line. These days there are lots of opportunities for working remotely, but you may have to think creatively, depending on your skills. If you need to work while traveling long-term, do some research and step outside that box. (More about working while traveling in Chapter 7.)

If you own a home, managing the property remotely can be a problem. My solution was to sell my home. Now, most of my posses-

"Pinch-Myself Moments" Blog

---

\* Read my blog essay "Pinch-Myself Moments" at CathleensOdyssey.com/**pinch-myself**

sions reside in a small storage space in Pahoa, Hawaii. I recognize that many people prefer to hold on to their homes. Some travelers prepare their home to be rented utilizing a property manager.

In many countries, your funds will stretch much further than in the United States or Europe. So, you don't have to be able to make a great deal of money to afford to travel. I have lived several places where my monthly expenses never exceeded $1000 USD.* (India, Kyrgyzstan, Sri Lanka, Malaysia, Indonesia, Ecuador.)

My first long-term trip was for 3½ months to Peru. That worked out for me. But I gave myself permission to return home if, at any time, I decided I was not enjoying the trip. If you have any misgivings, I recommend you try for four to six weeks for a first long-term trip.

My recent two-year journey was originally planned as a six-week trip to Spain to walk the Camino de Santiago. Then, I thought that as long as I was in Europe, I might as well go to some other places. By the time I left the US, I had plans for a six-to-eight-month trip to Europe. Before I knew it, I had been wandering around Europe for thirteen months and was ready to embark from Estonia to Kyrgyzstan. That trip got a little out of control. But it worked because I was fortunate enough to not have anything back in the United States pressing me to return.

> *My recent two-year journey was originally planned as a six-week trip to Spain...*

If you are going to travel long-term, I strongly suggest that you not try to move around every few days. Adopt the "slow travel" lifestyle, or you will most likely get burnt out quickly. Choose fewer locations and stay longer. This has the advantage of saving money in transportation costs—especially by air. You may also receive nice discounts for lodging when you plan to stay a month or more.

Most of the rest of this book provides lots of information on how to make a long-term travel lifestyle work.

If you are considering long term travel, my "Long-Term Travel Worksheet" may help you decide. You can download it at:
CathleensOdyssey.com/dpt-downloads

* This does not include airfare between the countries.

## WHAT IS RIGHT FOR YOU?

I am not saying that everyone should take on all these travel styles.

It is important for each person to figure out what his/her travel style is. It may take a while, and it may change from time to time, and place to place. Don't allow others (friends, travel acquaintances, tourist agencies, guides, or anything you read) determine what your travel style is. Don't feel guilty if you are not continuously meeting local people, experiencing all the sights, engaging in the culture. Pick and choose what works for you. (Journaling about it helps a lot!) And be careful not to choose to change your way of living too much all at once, or you risk becoming jaded or burned out.

The most important thing is to savor the experiences you do have.

# Chapter Two

# Planning is Half the Fun!

> **In this Chapter...**
> - Dream
> - Plan

## Dream

My trips (or the next destination) always begin with some day-dreaming. I start visualizing myself in some far-off destination. Something has inspired me, like someone's travelogue or a blog post. Or I have chosen a destination based on a personal interest or hobby. (For example, I chose countries in Europe—Scotland, Ireland, Netherlands, Estonia—based on the likelihood of finding other women who knit and spin.)

Then I start researching my destination and my reasons for the choice. What is the food like? What activities or attractions would I enjoy there? Who could I meet? After lots of reading, I begin narrowing down locations.

I rarely have time to visit all the places I would like to. It is impossible to experience all that a country has to offer. It is useful to read travel blogs about the destination. If I am having trouble deciding, I will sometimes journal about it. Writing down some visualizations starts to make the trip feel real. It also is helpful to write about the pros and cons of each place. (Is it easy to get to? big city or small town? good food? expensive? good places to stay? touristy or quiet? special attraction I want to visit?) Sometimes my budget makes the choice for me.

> **TIP**
> *A excellent resource for general information about almost any place in the world is **WIKITRAVEL.COM**. The entries may be a little outdated, but you can get some general information about the destination including local transportation, things to see and do, food, lodging, staying safe and more. The best part about these pages is the information about how to "Get in" and "Get out" of the destination via air, land, and sea. When using Wikitravel.com, it is important to double-check the information using another source that is up to date. Prices are almost always outdated, and businesses may have closed.*

During the Dream stage is a good time to start taking notes. One way of doing this is to use a word processing document or note-taking app (see "TIP" below) to store all the information and links you find. Within the document or app, categorize the information something like this:

- General Country information
  This includes such things as visa requirements, arrival airport information, currency and exchange rates, etc.
- Destinations I want to visit within the country
  - Activities and things to see
  - Lodging possibilities
  - Info on local transportation
  - Cafés and restaurants
  - Local tourism websites

Then, as I locate information on the Internet, I can cut, paste and edit. My documents are full of travel blog links. (They are also kind of messy, but that is okay—they are only for my reference.)

> **TIP**
> *I use Microsoft's OneNote app to keep track of this kind of information because the ability to categorize information is built in. Also, all my notes are automatically synced between my laptop and mobile devices, so I have the information available on the go. Similar note-taking apps include: Google Keep, Evernote, and Apple Notes. Of course, an old-fashioned paper notebook works, too.*

If I am traveling with a theme in mind, sometimes this means trying to contact locals BEFORE I decide on destinations. Social media helps with this. The responses from local contacts mostly

*Planning is Half the Fun*

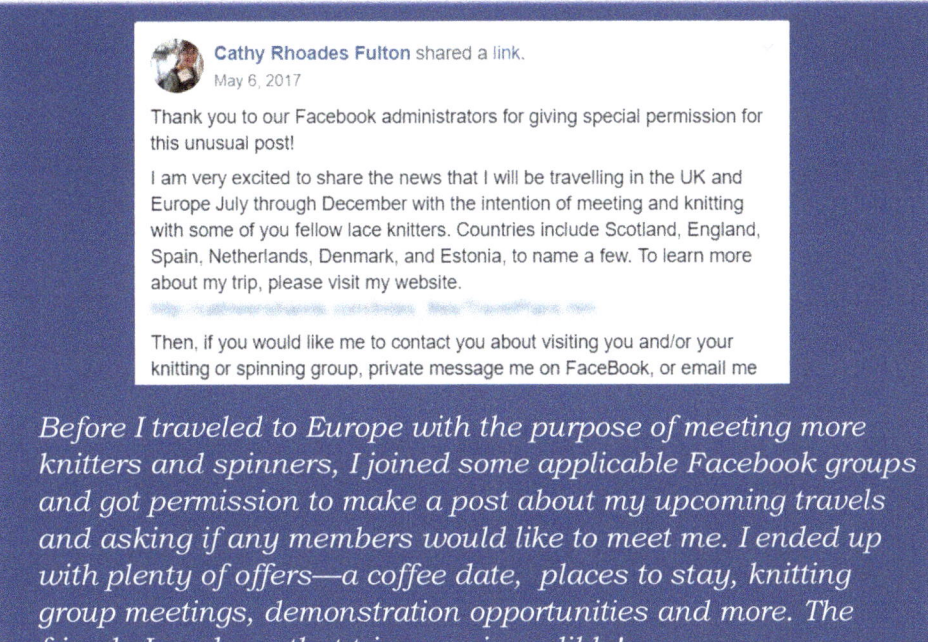

*Before I traveled to Europe with the purpose of meeting more knitters and spinners, I joined some applicable Facebook groups and got permission to make a post about my upcoming travels and asking if any members would like to meet me. I ended up with plenty of offers—a coffee date, places to stay, knitting group meetings, demonstration opportunities and more. The friends I made on that trip were incredible!*

determined my destinations. See more about Thematic Travel in Chapter 12.

Once I choose a destination, it is time to start the planning process.

## Plan

*Honing your skills for making your own travel plans and reservations is a core practice for becoming an experienced independent traveler.*

Before actually planning my trip and making reservations, I find out about the requirements to enter the country. If the visa process is complicated or expensive, for example, I may choose another destination.

Most countries require that your passport be valid for at least six months past your arrival date if you are entering the country as a tourist.

**Visas and Other Travel Documents**

The government tourism websites of the country you are planning to visit are a good start to learn about passport/visa/insurance/vaccination requirements. But make sure it is the government's official website. There are lots of private tourism sites

Dream. Plan. Travel.

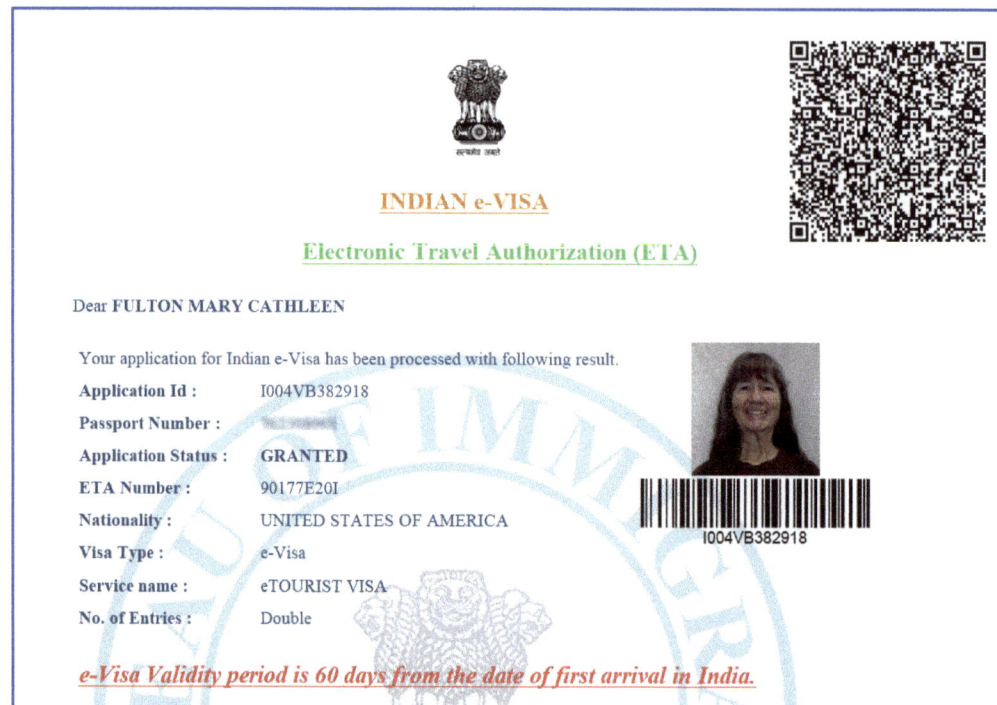

*The first visa I had to apply for in advance was for India. The on-line application required a .jpg image of my passport photo. Since I had one stored on my computer, the application procedure was straightforward and I received my approval within 24 hours.*

out there masquerading as the official site and they may have outdated information.

Entry requirements vary depending on the country you are from. If you are traveling with a United States passport, you can use the US State Department's international travel pages to find out requirements for US citizens. **Travel.State.Gov** is the website.

**It is up to you to find out if you need a visa in advance to enter a country.**

The visa application process varies, and may require you to mail your passport, so allow plenty of time to get travel documentation sorted out. Increasingly, many countries offer a way to easily apply and receive your visa online. But if the visa process is complicated, you might decide to hire an agency to acquire your visa for you.

Some countries do not require advance visas if you are traveling as a tourist. Your passport is merely stamped on arrival.

# Planning is Half the Fun

> *My visa to India was a snap to acquire on line. So was my 30-day entry visa to Sri Lanka. However, since I wanted to stay longer in Sri Lanka, I had to renew my visa. That process was much more involved and required a trip to the capital of Colombo. I decided the agency fee for handling the renewal was worth it.*

Be sure you are aware of activities you can engage in as a tourist. In some countries if you are doing mission work or journalism, for example, a special visa is required. Do not try get around these laws!

You will be limited on the time you can stay in the country. Make sure you know how long that is. In some places, overstaying your visa means a small fine; in others, you could end up in jail.

### TIP
*If you are transiting through (i.e. landing but not staying in) a country, find out if you will be required to go through immigration in that country in order to board your next flight. If so, do you need a transit visa? The airline can usually tell you.*

**It is also up to you to know what other documents you need.** Some requirements may include—but are not limited to—proof of immunizations, travel insurance, and proof of return or onward travel—i.e. proof you are leaving the country before your visa will expire.*

Some destinations require specific vaccinations for foreign visitors. You can check with the Center for Disease Control's "Destinations" page to learn about recommended and required immunizations. WWWNC.CDC.GOV/TRAVEL/DESTINATIONS/LIST (Or search for "CDC destinations" in your web browser). If you are going to be traveling for an extended period, a pre-travel check-up with your physician is the best way to find out which immunizations are right for you.

---

\* If you are entering most countries as a tourist, they will require some kind of proof that you are going to leave. Usually this means an air, bus, train, or other kind of ticket. But you may not know when or where you are going after leaving the country you are getting ready to enter. Travel bloggers Goats on the Road have written an excellent article helping you with this dilemma. "7 Ways to Provide Proof of Onward Travel." WWW.GOATSONTHEROAD.COM/7-WAYS-PROVIDE-PROOF-ONWARD-TRAVEL/

**Steps I Take on the Road to a Reservation**

Slowly I narrow down my destination choices and (taking a deep breath) I start making reservations.

Other travelers often ask me how I research my trips. One person even asked if she could look over my shoulder while I planned my next trip. So, here are my methods for making plans to move on to my next destination. On-line resources that I use are listed in the table on page 42.

> **TIP**
> *Before I begin my research, I set up some way to take notes and keep track of information. You can use a pen and paper, but if you open a blank text document, or use a note-taking app, like OneNote or Evernote, it is easy to cut and paste websites and schedules, edit, make comments, and then finalize your schedule into a workable itinerary.*

**1. Get reservations for lodging FIRST.** If you don't have lodging reserved and schedule your transportation first, you might then discover that there are no lodging choices available for your arrival date. You can read more about choosing your lodging in Chapter 6.

**2. Decide how to travel.** I begin by finding out the best ways to get there from my previous location (air? train? boat?) Ask fellow travelers and guesthouse hosts for their suggestions. I check schedules and prices and start keeping notes for the more promising itineraries.

I love to travel by train and will usually choose it over a bus, even if it is a little more expensive. When traveling VERY long distances, air may be the most sensible choice. Sometimes it is quite a bit cheaper to fly than to travel by train, boat or bus. For example, it would have been cheaper for me to fly from San Sebastian, Spain to Amsterdam, but I

> *I LOVE trains for so many reasons: stations are usually located in town centers; rarely are there security checks, show up at the station 10 minutes before departure, carry on everything and have all your stuff available to you during the trip (even a bottle of wine if you so desire!), wide seats—sometimes you even get a table, reasonable legroom, easy to walk around, scenery, low-carbon footprint, AND I can have my knitting!! I am often not ready for the journey to end.*

# Planning is Half the Fun

cherished the opportunity to take a high-speed train. You can read about this experience at CATHLEENSODYSSEY.COM/fly-across-france

**3. Create your itinerary.** This the longest step, especially if you are trying to balance trip duration, complexity, and cost.

When opting for ground transportation, I start with GOOGLE MAPS or ROME2RIO.COM and plug in my origin and destination. This gives me an idea of what kinds of conveyances are available. (Use these with caution because sometimes the information is outdated—but it is a starting point.)

If I am flying, I usually start with KIWI.COM or ORBITZ.COM. Recently, Kiwi seemed to provide cheaper alternatives. Be careful when choosing flights. Check to see if you have to pay for your checked bags (And now, increasingly, your carry-on bags may also have a surcharge.) A flight that looks more expensive may offer a free checked bag and your overall fare may be cheaper.

When looking at flight schedules, if one option is significantly cheaper than others, be sure you don't have an 18-hour layover somewhere or something worse. You will either sleep in the airport (ugh!) or you may only have expensive options for nearby lodging . Some itineraries may have you transfer to a different airport in a city resulting in an unexpected taxi fare of $100 US or more. (This is not unusual for flights going through New York City.)

### TIP
*Remember when comparing airfare with bus or train fare to add the cost of transportation to and from airports, as well as add-on fees like checked bags.*

### TIP
*It is not unusual for me to spend several days debating over long-distance flights. As a result, a lot of "cookies" get stored in my browser alerting the search engines of my interest in that itinerary and the ticket prices seem to increase. I have discovered that it does help to occasionally clear out my cookies between searches. (Search for "clear cookies" in your browser's address bar to see how to do this in your browser.)*

**4. Decide how to travel to and from airport/bus/train stations.** This goes for traveling from origin (current) lodgings to the departure airport or station, *and* from the destination airport or station to your lodgings. Lodging hosts can usually help but be careful.

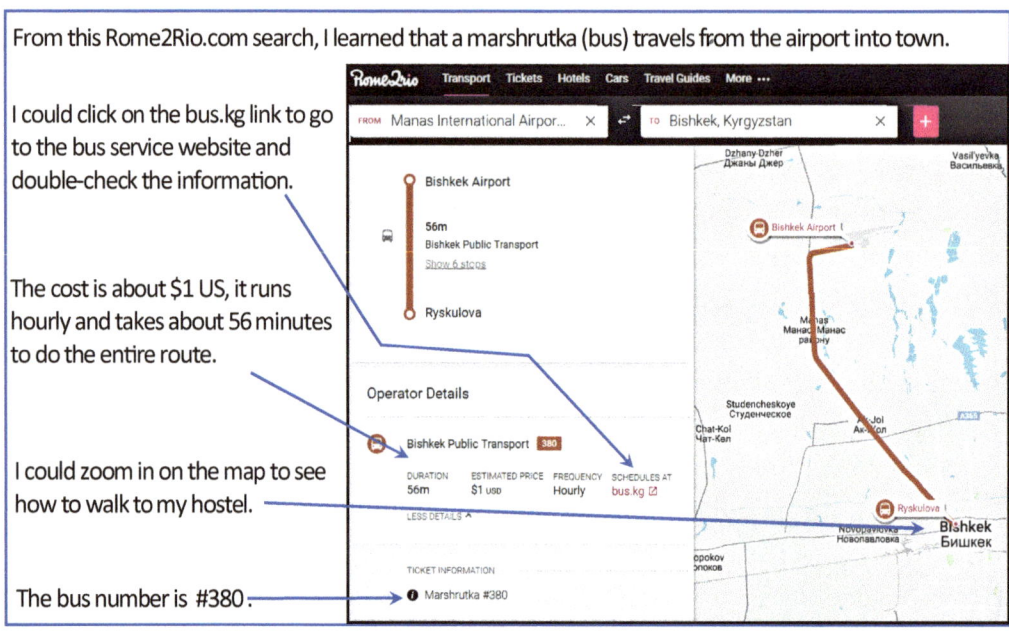

From this Rome2Rio.com search, I learned that a marshrutka (bus) travels from the airport into town.

I could click on the bus.kg link to go to the bus service website and double-check the information.

The cost is about $1 US, it runs hourly and takes about 56 minutes to do the entire route.

I could zoom in on the map to see how to walk to my hostel.

The bus number is #380.

There may be an inexpensive bus to the airport and hotel staff may only offer you the option of a taxi.

Airport websites often have a page showing transfer options from airport to city centers.

Google maps is my number one resource for locating transportation options within a city. For example, when I arrived in Utrecht, I already had downloaded maps for bus and walking directions to my hostel, so I knew the options when I arrived.

If Google does not provide bus directions, try **ROME2RIO.COM**. When I was planning my trip to Bishkek, Kyrgystan, Rome2Rio.com showed me the map above of the bus route from the airport to the stop that was only a few blocks from my hostel. Because I had done this research, I saved about $10.00 US because I did not take a taxi.

**5. Collect all confirmations and directions.** Once you have purchased your tickets and made lodging reservations, collect all the confirmations, maps, directions to and from lodgings, etc. in one place. Ticket details are usually emailed to you. I save each one in a separate file. Usually I create a .pdf version of the email if there is no .pdf confirmation attached. Then I load them onto my mobile device. To make it easy to find all my confirmations while on the go, I place a shortcut to each one on my home screen and place

## Planning is Half the Fun

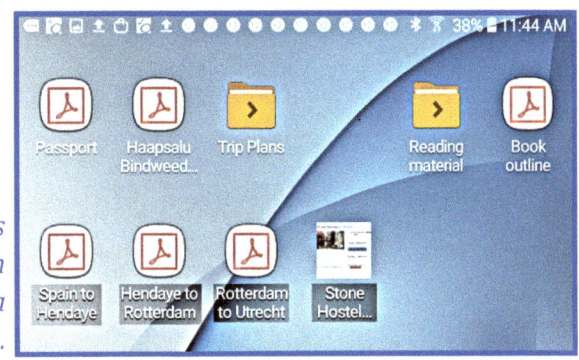

*All my confirmations and e-tickets are literally at my fingertips when I store them on my tablet with a shortcut to them on my home screen.*

them on the screen in chronological order and with meaningful filenames. When I arrive at the airport or station, I have all the information I need to get paper boarding passes or tickets.

### WARNING
*Sometimes airlines require you to have a paper copy of your boarding pass when you arrive at the airport. (Or they will charge you some exorbitant fee to print it.) Be sure to check on this in advance. Often, your host will print these for a nominal fee or can direct you to a nearby copy center.*

Copies of my passport and other documents I might need (like visas, etc.) are also already on my mobile device, for quick reference.

**6. Download local maps to your mobile device.** Utilize Google Maps' "Offline Maps" option to download a map of your next destination. Then, when you arrive, if you don't have access to the Internet, you can still get around.

### ADVICE
*Send your itinerary to a family member or friend. Promise to let someone know when you have reached your destination.*

You can read a step-by-step example of the above methods in action on my blog post, "Trip Planning Technique: San Sebastian to Utrecht" at CATHLEENSODYSSEY.COM/planning-Spain-Netherlands.

Trip Planning Technique

### TIP
*Have a Plan B. If you have concerns that something might go wrong with your plans, keep "plan B" information handy. For example, is the connection time between a bus and train a little bit short? Next train isn't until the next day? Keep a list of hostels and guesthouses that are near the connecting station on your mobile device, along with a map showing where they are.*

## WEBSITES I USE FOR PLANNING

As you become more experienced in making your own travel plans, you will develop a list of websites and apps that work well for you. Here are the ones I currently find useful:

**LODGING:** For hostels, I use Hosteling International (**HIHOSTELS.COM**) or **HOSTELWORLD.COM**. For guesthouses, I mostly use **BOOKING.COM**. A similar site to Booking.com is **AGODA.COM**. Booking.com usually presents you with locations that have dorm rooms, but you can easily filter them out if you prefer private rooms. Keep in mind that many hostels now offer private rooms as well as dorm rooms.

**AIR TRAVEL:** I used **ORBITZ.COM** almost exclusively for a long time, but recently I have found that **KIWI.COM** seems to find better fares.

**TRAIN TRAVEL:** I usually start with **ROME2RIO.COM** to get an idea of the possible routes and find the websites of the train companies.

Before I book train tickets, I always check **SEAT61.COM** for detailed information on just about any train system in the world. Mark Smith, also known as "The Man in Seat 61," provides more about train travel than you will ever need. Because of the great service Mark provides for free, I always try to purchase train tickets through the links on his site, because he earns a small commission with each purchase.

**BUS AND BOAT TRAVEL:** Again, start with **ROME2RIO.COM.** Then follow the links to carriers' websites.

**MAPS:** Google Maps. I don't use a cell phone, so when I am away from wifi, I utilize Google Maps' "Offline Maps" feature. I can download a detailed map of the area I will travel to and be ready to find my way as soon as I arrive. (Some people prefer **MAPS.ME**.)

**FINDING ROUTES AND CONVEYANCES:** I try Google Maps first, but often they do not show local bus schedules. Then I turn to **ROME2RIO.COM**.

**TAXIS:** **UBER** is available in many countries. **GRAB** is a similar service offered in Southeast Asia. Both services are beginning to provide dispatch counters in some airports.

| | Operator: | MNC | MNC | RM | RM | MNC | MNC | MNC | MNC | MNC | MNC | RM | RM | MNC |
|---|---|---|---|---|---|---|---|---|---|---|---|---|---|---|
| | Days Operated: | Sound of Barra Ferry Request Mon - Sat | School Holiday | Schoolday | Schoolday | Monday to Saturday | Monday to Saturday | Monday to Saturday | Monday to Friday | Saturday | Saturday | Schoolday | Schoolday Monday to Thursday | Monday to Saturday |
| **Stops** | | | | | | | | | | | | | | |
| Castlebay School | | | | | | [0832] | 1018 | | [1322] | | 1355 | 1450 | 1540 | 1630d |
| Castlebay PO/Pier | | 0625a | 0750a | | | 0830 | 1025 | | 1320 | | 1405 | | | 1635d |
| Castlebay Square | | | | | | | | | | | 1406 | 1451 | 1541 | 1636d |
| Glen RE/Garrygall | | a | | | | | 1026 | | | | 1407 | 1453 | 1542 | 1637d |
| Brevig R.E | | a | | | | | 1030 | | | | 1410 | 1458 | 1545 | 1640d |
| Earsary | | a | | | | | 1031 | | | | 1411 | 1502 | 1548 | 1641d |
| Bruernish Village | | a | | | | | B | | | | | 1508r | 1552r | |
| I.O.B Hotel / Tangasdale | | a | 0754a | | | 0834 | | | 1324 | | | | | |
| Borve Junction | | a | 0755a | | | 0835 | | | 1325v | | | | | |
| Craigstone R.E | | a | 0756a | | | 0836 | | | 1326 | | | | | |
| Grean & Cleat R.E | | a | 0800a | | | 0840 | | | 1330 | | | | | |
| Northbay Church | | a | 0804a | | | 0844 | 1040 | | 1334 | | 1420 | 1515 | 1554 | 1650d |
| Ardveenish R.E | | a | | | | 0845 | 1041 | | 1335 | | 1421 | 1517 | 1555 | 1651d |

**Barra Bus Timetable** — Operated by Macneil Coaches (MNC) 075060 72309 & R Macmillan (RM) 01871 890366

*Example of a challenging bus schedule on the Isle of Barra in the Outer Hebrides. It is not helpful that there is no route map so you can figure out where those bus stops are.*

**Note for all readers:**

I really do enjoy all aspects of planning. For me, it is like a puzzle to be solved. There have been times when I have spent several hours working out all the ins and outs for an excursion only to find that there was no way for me to be transported on one essential leg of the trip. A disappointment, but I usually don't mind so much. I was just not able to solve that puzzle. I go on to the next idea (and puzzle).

*Detailed travel planning is not for everybody!* If this kind of thing makes you crazy or is likely to frustrate you, there is nothing wrong with getting some help from a guide or agency. But it is helpful to have some basic travel planning skills, in case you get stuck or something goes amiss.

---

*When my daughter and I were planning to hike to Choquequirao in Peru, I spent a great deal of time trying to figure out how to do the trek independently of a guide. It is possible, but after doing quite a bit of research, I decided I did not want to worry about all the aspects of hiring horses for our equipment, getting permits, renting equipment, acquiring and preparing food, etc. We hired a guide and were so glad we did. It was the most glamorous camping trip I ever went on: tents were set up, food was prepared, all our gear was transported, and we became great friends with the guide—even to this day. Yes, it cost much more than I usually budget for travel, but it was one of the most memorable and empowering experiences I have had.*

# CHAPTER THREE

# ON THE MOVE

**IN THIS CHAPTER...**

- Stay Organized
- Checklist for Moving On
- At My Fingertips
- On Arrival
- Long-Haul Survival Guide

The day has arrived. You are movin' on to your next destination. Or maybe it's the first! For many people the days they spend moving from one place to the next are the most stressful of any trip. However if you have made detailed plans and follow a few "movin' on" tips, the travel day might be as much fun as the rest of the journey.

## STAY ORGANIZED

Having a set routine when making a major move from place to place has its advantages:

- It will keep you focused on schedules and where you need to be—especially when changing planes/trains/buses.
- It will turn you into a confident traveler and make you feel empowered.
- When asked for documentation, like passports, reservations, tickets, etc, you will have them at your fingertips.
- You will be less disoriented when you arrive at your destination.
- You will save money—sometimes, quite a bit of money.

◀ *On the move: Taking the ferry from Santoña to Laredo on the northern coast of Spain.*

When moving from place to place, I always have exactly three things to keep track of: my backpack, a daypack and my waist bag. Everything else is packed in one of these—and each item has its place. If I sit down in the train station and eat or write in my journal, I pack everything in its place before getting up. As I take a few steps from the seat, I turn around and look to be sure I did not leave anything.

## Checklist for Moving On

If you have done most of the steps outlined in Chapter 2, you will be prepared to have a smooth transition into your travel day (or days). This checklist will send you on your way.

- Do all the steps listed under "Plan" in Chapter 2.
- Plan for what food you will take for traveling (or have a sure knowledge of what food will be available on the way). Plan when you will prepare it. If you have an early train to catch, you should probably prepare your lunch and snacks the night before.
- Packing: If you depart early in the morning, pack the night before. If flying, make sure all items that are not allowed through airport security are in your checked baggage.

> *I have lost two Swiss Army knives because I failed to move them from my waist bag to my checked baggage before moving on.*

- Plan your time schedule for leaving your lodgings so you are not late arriving at the station/airport. Write it down. Set alarms. Arrange a taxi if you are using one. If you are

# On the Move

taking a bus to the station/airport, make sure you know exactly how and where to board it. You don't want to start off late on your trip!

- Find out the exchange rate for the currency in your new country. Decide before you leave how much money to withdraw at the ATM in the destination airport or station. Most places (including guesthouses and shops) in developing countries do not accept credit cards, so you will need plenty of cash to pay for your expenses for at least the first few days. If you know before you arrive how much to withdraw, you will (1) be sure you have enough money in your account, and (2) not be trying to figure out the local exchange rate while standing in front of the ATM.

*TIP*
*When using an ATM, it is best to look like*
*you know exactly what you are doing.*
*Get in and out as quickly as possible.*

**Movin' On Checklist**

*Use this template to customize your own checklist each time you travel to your next destination.*

- ☐ Plans completed:
    - ☐ Visa, if required (hardcopy printed if needed)
    - ☐ Lodging Reservation(s) for:
        *(list)*
    - ☐ Tickets to:
        *(list destinations)*
    - ☐ How much money to withdraw at destination ATM (in local currency): _____
- ☐ Download to mobile device (with shortcut on home screen)
    - ☐ Offline Maps of destination
    - ☐ Visas (if required)
    - ☐ All reservations/tickets/confirmations on mobile device
    - ☐ Schedule for traveling to station/airport
    - ☐ Proof of onward or return travel (for immigration)
    - ☐ Entertainment for trip (ebooks, videos, etc.)
- ☐ Food for trip packed
    *(Food list goes here)*
- ☐ Pack
    *(List of items that are not allow through security are in checked bags.)*
    *(Other packing reminders—things not to forget.)*

I keep a generic checklist template similar to this on my computer and then as I make my plans, I copy and edit the template as needed. You can download a "Movin' On" checklist that you can edit in your word processor at: **CathleensOdyssey.com/dpt-downloads**

Movin' On Checklist

## At My Fingertips

Rummaging through purse and packs to find something that you almost always need in route is frustrating and time-consuming. Over time, you learn what to pack in the top or outside pockets of your carry-on bag. Anticipate what you will need while in your seat and place those things in your purse or a smaller bag that will fit by your feet or under the seat in front of you.

For example, I usually bring my own food to eat on a flight. My food bag won't fit in my waist bag, the "personal item" that I use as a kind of purse. But I pack it in the top of my carry-on daypack so I can pull it out right before I stow the pack in the overhead bin and sit down. (Same goes for my water bottle.) Then the food bag and bottle goes under the seat in front of me along with my waist bag—ready for take-off.

In Chapter 8, I show you what I carry in my waist bag, which I use in lieu of a purse.

### On My Mobile Device

I am not sure how I used to travel without my tablet, which is my only mobile device. I can store so much information and entertainment on it. For example, here are the files I download to my tablet when getting ready to move from place to place:

- Confirmation of all reservations for the trip:
  - Plane, bus, rail, and/or boat-to-airport transfers
  - Lodging reservations

> **TIP**
> *When changing countries, be sure to have the name, address, and phone number of your lodging easily available. You may be asked for it in Immigration.*

- Confirmation of Visa(s) (if an advanced visa is required for the country I am visiting or transiting through)
  Some countries may require a hardcopy version. Make sure of the requirements and that you meet them several days before you leave. Don't be scrambling to find a printer on your day of travel. The airline won't let you on the plane if you don't have the required documentation.
- Proof of onward travel if you are arriving in a new country. (See page 37 for more about this.)

On the Move

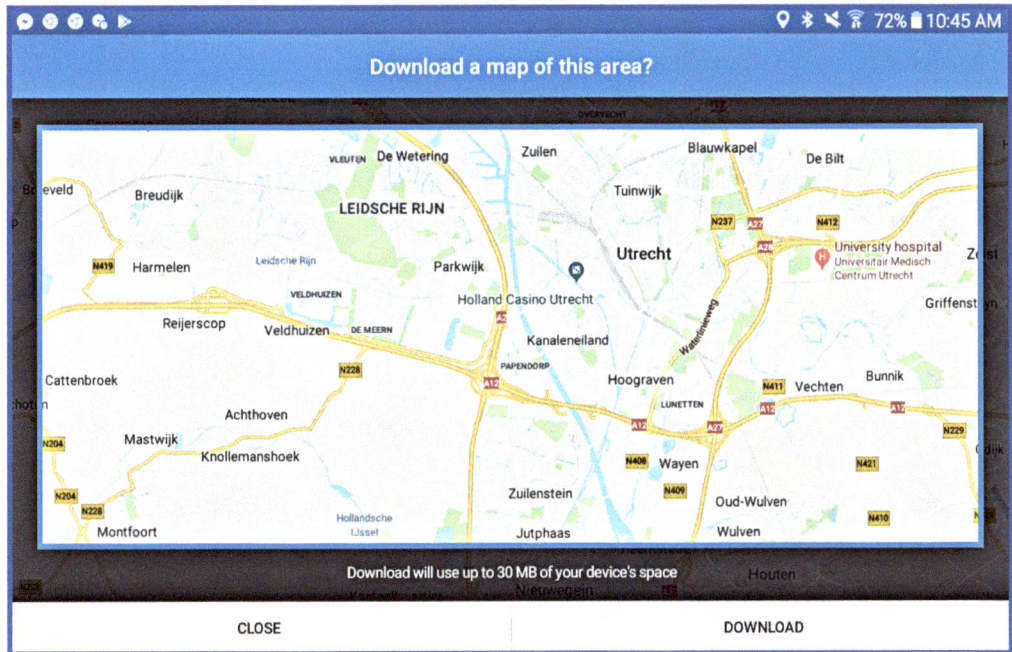

*The download page for Google Maps' offline map.*

- Ebook/Audio Book/Video for en-route entertainment.
- Offline map of destination
  As mentioned in the previous chapter, I download an offline version of Google Maps for the area I will be staying in. To do this, you will have to install the GoogleMaps app onto your mobile device. (This is not necessary if you are sure you will have mobile access as soon as you reach your destination.)

  > TIP
  > *If you plan to walk from the bus/train station to your lodging, take a screenshot image of the directions from the arrival port or terminal to your lodging before you leave—just in case the off-line version of Google maps decides not to work. This has happened to me and I was glad I had that backup in a strange town.*

## ON ARRIVAL

When arriving by air to a new country, here is the gauntlet you will have to get through:

1. Immigration
   Be sure to get in the correct line! Be prepared with your

*Delhi's immigration hall is full of light and art.*

passport, any visas or other documents that are required, address/phone number of where you be staying, and proof of onward travel.

2. Bag Claim followed by Customs
Sometimes you are given a declarations document while you are on the plane, so you have plenty of time to study it. If not, be sure to read any signs in the customs area of the arrival hall, so you don't inadvertently bring contraband into the country.

3. The Public Arrival Hall
This can be a bit overwhelming. Take your time to adjust to your surroundings. Don't let taxi-drivers and other hawkers distract you.

### TIP
*Finding the restroom will probably fit in here somewhere! Freshen up a bit. If the climate is quite different from where you came from, you may want to change into more comfortable clothing. Of course, you packed them in your carry-on or in the top of your checked bag, right?*

- Find the ATM and get cash. If there is a place to change some of your cash into small change, like a bank kiosk or money-changer, do so.

## On the Move

> **TIP**
> *You need cash in most developing countries—few shops, guesthouses, or cafés take cards. Learn how to always carry small change because almost no one can change small bills. (Sometimes a shopkeeper may take your large bill and disappear out the door without explanation. They are going to see if any of their neighbors have change. Don't worry, they will be right back.)*

- If you need a local SIM card for your cell phone, the arrival hall is a convenient place to buy one. Then your phone will be usable immediately.
- Locate your planned mode of transportation to your lodgings. (You researched it earlier, right?) Otherwise, see if there is a visitor's information desk to inquire about transportation.

> *Here is how I saved money because I was organized when I hit the ground in Biskek, Kyrgyzstan. I was aware that the taxi drivers at the airport would pounce as I entered the arrival hall, and they were ready with their "tourist prices." Because I had done the research beforehand, I knew that there was a bus that would take me within blocks from my hostel for about $1 US. (See page 40.) I even knew where to look for the bus when I exited the airport. When the taxi drivers descended on me, I had my answer to deter them. One driver tried to tell me that the buses were dangerous and I would get my waist bag stolen—he even jerked on my pack while he spoke! But I had done my research and knew that the buses were perfectly safe and I walked confidently to the bus stand. Total saved: about $10.00 USD.*

If my lodging is located a reasonable distance from the bus or train station, and if I am not completely exhausted, I often opt to walk rather than take a bus or taxi. (This is one of many reasons I pack light.) I think my main motivation for walking is that I am *so darn cheap*. But walking also gives me a chance to stretch my legs and get a little exercise and fresh air. I get acquainted with the neighborhood, maybe even purchasing some food to eat from a corner store. I might get a cup of tea in a little café and relax a bit. I also feel a little bit like I know what I am doing when I tell those pesky taxi drivers, "No, I am walking!"

Dream. Plan. Travel.

> *Sometimes, I will email my host in advance and ask how much I should pay for a taxi from the station. There are often "local" fares and "tourist" fares. I don't mind paying a little more than locals, but not three times as much. One time my host said the taxi should cost no more than $2 US. When I arrived at the bus station, taxi drivers laid siege. I asked how much; they said $7; I countered with $4 (giving in a lot, in my mind.) He would not budge from $5. I announced, "I'll walk," and I strutted away to walk four kilometers in the heat. I was certainly glad I had packed light that day.*

### TIP

*Often when I arrive in my new lodgings, my first impression is that I don't like the place; I don't want to stay there; I want to go back to my previous place; etc. Then I start looking for things that are wrong with the place. This is normal; I have heard that this phenomenon affects other travelers. The feeling can be especially overwhelming if you are tired when you arrive.*

*My antidote is to tell myself, "Wait until tomorrow to decide what you want to do." You usually get used to the new surroundings, meet people, or just get some rest by then and the world looks better.*

*However, if, after a couple days you feel the same way, you may enjoy your destination more if you find a different place to stay. (I did change hostels in Utrecht, where I had found myself stuffed in a crowded dorm room with four young girls who chattered and primped all night, like they were in a slumber party. (This was an unusual occurrence, however.)*

## LONG-HAUL SURVIVAL GUIDE

Do you have a long journey ahead of you? One that takes more than one day? Or a series of long-haul flights (over six hours) and layovers? Read the Cathleen's Odyssey Travel Handbook article, "Long-Flight Survival Guide." In it you will find a long list of special tips for turning something you probably dread into an adventure. Tips like:

- Planning and seat selection
- Preparing for arrival before you leave
- Preparing yourself mentally
- Staying comfortable
- How to pack a long-haul survival kit

# On the Move

- Fun "keeping-in-touch" activities to do in route
- Taking advantage of long layovers
- Dealing with security lines
- Taking care of yourself in the days after the journey

The Long-Flight Survival Guide can be found at:

**CathleensOdyssey.com/long-flight-survival-guide**

Included in the article is a download that shows you how to create your own "Long-Flight Survival Kit."

You can also read a blog post about how I turned what could have been a grueling 50-hour journey from Indonesia to Ecuador into an adventure at: **CathleensOdyssey.com/drudgery-adventure**

Long Flight Survival Guide

Turning Drudgery into Adventure

### Cutting the Queue

*When I arrived in Bilbao, Spain from the UK, there were two signs—one for EU citizens and one that said "All others." Apparently everyone else on my plane carried EU documentation, so I was surprised and hesitant to walk to the front of the "All others" line. I felt like I was "cutting!"*

*Eventually I tentatively began my way through the cordoned maze. All at once, from an immigration officer's desk came a shout…"No! NO! NO!" and he gestured me to the back of the EU line. While I was asking other travelers what I should do, the officer stomped up and asked gruffly, "De donde estas?" I showed him my passport. He grudgingly pointed to the "All others" area and stomped back to his seat, while I wound myself through the empty maze of queue-line ribbons, very conscious of 200 pairs of eyes watching me from the "EU line." I was the next person to go through immigration. Now I knew I was cutting in line! The officer's stamp came down sharply on my passport and I was released into the baggage claim area. I could not wait to grab my pack and slink out, disappearing in the chaotic arrival hall.*

*My entrance pass to Spain. The permission I needed to start the Camino de Santiago del Norte!*

# Chapter Four

# A Penny Saved...

> **In this Chapter...**
> - 16 Ways I Save Money When Traveling
> - Do Your Own Research
> - Always Know Where Your Money is Going
> - Saving on Lodging
> - Saving on Transportation

I am, by nature, a person who watches where her money is spent. Some friends and family members have gone so far as to label me "cheap" and "penny-pinching." However, if I had not watched those pennies/rupees/soles/soms over the past few years, I would no longer be able to hop around the world the way I do.

Being a frugal independent traveler has quite a few benefits. You have to be creative and flexible in choosing your activities. But usually this means interacting with locals much more often than you would on a guided tour. When you ask your host or someone in a café or on the street for directions, information, or suggestions, you will often become engaged in an enjoyable conversation. You may learn about opportunities that the guided tourist will never experience. Sometimes you will receive offers of hospitality, like home-cooked meals, invitations to weddings and parties, or a place to sleep. As a result, your experiences become richer, deeper.

> *One time, when I was about twelve years old, my younger sister and I rushed home to show Daddy, "Look what we got for free!"*
>
> *He quipped, "Well you should have looked around for something cheaper." I got half my DNA from that man—and it shows!*

Independent travelers have quite a bit of leeway in how and where they spend their money. There are many, many places in the world (especially in Asia, Africa, and South and Central America) in which it is inexpensive to travel just because the cost of living is low. But I also spent 13 months in Europe during 2017-18 for less than $1,300 USD per month using the tips in this chapter.

Dream. Plan. Travel.

## 16 Ways I Save Money When Traveling

1. I start with a travel budget and record every penny I spend. You can learn more about how I keep track of my spending in "Always Know Where Your Money is Going" below.

2. I prepare many of my own meals.
   If you are not really into preparing most of your own meals, at least carry a few food-preparation essentials (like a hot water heater, cup, bowl, thermos, etc.) Also carry tea bags/instant coffee, oatmeal, and some instant soups. You will learn a lot more about this in Chapter 5.

3. I take my time when arriving in a new country to get my bearings. Being rushed to jump in a taxi as soon as you clear customs usually results in an overpriced ride to the city center. Slow down, take a breath, ignore the hoard of taxi drivers, ask questions at the information desk, stop for a coffee, get your bearings. You can read my suggestions for doing so at:
   **CathleensOdyssey.com/taxi-paparazzi**

Dealing with Airport Taxi Paparazzi

4. I make financial transactions in the local currency.
   When using a credit card, if you have a choice of local or home currency, select the local currency. You will almost always get a better exchange rate.

5. I try to find ATMs (cash machines) that do not charge a transaction fee.
   If that is not possible, I usually opt to withdraw as much cash as I think I will need for a week or more, so I only pay the fee a minimal number of times.

6. I use public transportation as much as possible.
   See "Saving on Transportation" below.

7. I often stay in hostel dorm rooms.
   They are not just for 20-somethings! And there are other advantages. See Chapter 6 and "Saving on Lodging" below.

8. I travel thematically—meeting people and having experiences instead of visiting expensive attractions. See "Thematic Travel" in Chapter 12.

9. I am selective about the sites I do visit. Then, because I am so interested, I often stay all day and get my money's worth! See "Do Your Own Research" below.

*Having a theme to your travels means you meet other people who are passionate about the same things you are. My Dutch friend Connie (right) traveled with me in Estonia and we met many famous lace knitting designers, including Helen Poldve, who had recently designed a lace shawl for the queen of The Netherlands!*

10. I look for "free" city walking tours. These are available in many places. Check with the tourism office when you arrive. There is an expectation that you tip the guide at the end of the tour, based on what you decide the tour is worth.

    *The best free walking tour I have taken was the Harry Potter tour in Edinburgh, Scotland—the place where J.K. Rowling wrote her brilliant series.*

11. I look for discounts.
    Some of the organizations to which you belong offer discounts worldwide. If you are under 26 or over 55 years old, you will probably find many lodging and transportation discounts. Admission to many sights and attractions provide discounts to seniors and students. I was pleasantly surprised to discover that I could purchase a Senior Railcard in the United Kingdom that would save me 30% on almost all my train travel.

12. When making one-way reservations for transportation, I check to see if a round trip ticket is cheaper. Then I just don't use the return portion.

13. I limit the purchase of souvenirs.
    Collect memories, friends, experiences, and photos instead. Keep a journal—in 10 years it will be much more precious to you and your family than anything you buy in a gift shop. If

you are perusing craft and souvenir markets for gifts or keepsakes, use my method (below) for attending markets and fairs of all kinds. It takes a little longer, but I rarely go over budget.

14. I usually wash my clothes a few at a time in my room.
    Laundry costs can mount up. When laundry is provided free by your lodging, take advantage of it.

15. I embrace low-season travel.
    Yes, many sites are closed or have diminished hours. It can be cold (or very hot) in some locations. But you many find some deep discounts. I often received 20-25% off the already reduced low-season rate in hostels in Ireland and Scotland. There are other benefits: See "Low Season Travel" in Chapter 9.

16. I don't plan my next destination at the last minute.
    If you start researching transportation and lodging at least three to four weeks (or more) ahead, you have time to watch for and find discounts and look for reduced fares.

### CATHY'S FOOL-PROOF METHOD FOR SHOPPING IN MARKETS AND FAIRS

*(Caution: Requires discipline!)*

Before visiting the market or fair, make a list or notes about what you are looking for. Set a spending limit.

Once at the market, walk through most or all of the aisles of vendors one time through without purchasing anything. Keep your camera and notepad busy recording any items that catch your eye along with prices. What is special about it? Which vendor is selling it. How much does it cost? Do you like the vendor?

Retreat to a café for a snack or lunch and go over your list thinking about which items you really want to purchase. What will its use be? If it is a gift, will the recipient really like it?

Make a few wise choices and maybe a few frivolous ones, or prioritize the list. Add up the total cost. If you are over budget, make some cuts, or consider bargaining with the vendor.

Once you are under budget, the fun begins. You can return to the market and make your purchases.

As a result of using this method for many years, I have left festivals and markets with some pretty incredible finds and no remorse the next day.

*A Penny Saved...*

I have one other suggestion, which I rarely take advantage of because I already work remotely while traveling. This is to take part in work-exchange opportunities. Often for about 20 hours of work a week, you will be provided room and, sometimes, board. There can be other perks, like learning a new skill or free use of facilities. The jobs can be anything: cleaning rooms, farm and garden work, food preparation, teaching English, working with animals—you name it. If you have a special skill that you enjoy performing, look for opportunities to use it. Work exchanges can last from a week to several months.

A couple of websites to check are **Workaway.info** and Worldwide Opportunities on Organic Farms (**Wwoof.net**). You can also google, "travel work exchange" for more options as well as many blog posts about how this kind of travel works.

### TIP
*Be leery of some "voluntourism" organizations that require you to pay a large fee up front for lodging, meals, and donations to the organization. Some are reputable, but it is easy to find a work exchange (including for charitable organizations) without paying for the privilege. Sometimes you can just turn up in a location and ask if help is needed.*

## Do Your Own Research

If you rely on tourism offices for advice on restaurants, transportation, or local attractions, they will often only point you to those places which are members of the tourism organization or have paid for advertising. They may offer only the all-inclusive excursions and seem to know nothing of how you would go about doing the same trip on your own, much cheaper, and at your own pace. Sometimes they even try to talk you out of such an idea. One time, when I asked about walking trails in the nearby countryside, the tourism assistant looked at me like I was from another planet.

*Doing your own research ahead of time...will put you ahead of the game.*

Doing your own research ahead of time by reading articles and travel blogs will put you ahead of the game. Ask your host or other local about the best places to eat and how to use the bus system. I often use **WikiTravel.com** to learn about the sights, transportation options, and food of destinations I am considering. (The entries may be a little outdated, but I like using it as a starting point for further research.)

*Choose local sights based on your interests...*
*Don't follow the crowds to just any tourist attraction.*

Visit the websites of the attractions, museums, and other local sights. There have been several occasions that I have done so and then decided that I probably would not really enjoy the sight or that my money would be better spent elsewhere. And the reverse has been true. For example, at first, I was not entirely excited about going to the Titanic Museum in Belfast. But a visit to their website made it apparent that it would probably be worthwhile. I also found out that I was eligible for a discount since I was over 60. I ended up spending a full day there and was one of the last to leave.

TIP
*When visiting a large attraction, plan to arrive when it opens. The crowds are usually lighter early in the day. But, more importantly, if you end up really enjoying yourself, you will have the entire day to do so.*

## ALWAYS KNOW WHERE YOUR MONEY IS GOING

**Develop a travel budget before you leave home.**
While doing preliminary research for destinations, find out approximately what you can expect to pay for meals, lodging and transportation. Here are some ways to do that:
- Google "cost of traveling (country name)." Make sure any links you choose are recent (preferably written within the last year or so).
- Use a guesthouse or hostel booking site (like Booking.com or AirBnB) to plug in some planned destinations and dates to get an idea of your lodging costs.
- Use Google maps to find cafés and restaurants at your destination. Check the reviewer photos to look at menu images or visit a sampling of café sites to see if they post menus. This will give you an idea of food costs.
- If you are planning bus or train journeys, visit the websites for the train and bus companies to get an idea of fares.

# A Penny Saved...

Remember to add in your expected airfares, admission fees, and incidental costs, like gifts, personal care items, etc.

See my original hand-written budget planning notes for my first trip to Peru on page 54.

This may all sound like a lot of trouble, but it will prevent expensive surprises once you are on your trip.

**Record all your expenditures**

For most people, just having to write down all expenditures provides an incentive to spend less. By keeping track, you can allow the occasional splurge in one category when you see that you have saved money in another.

I like to use an Excel or Google spreadsheet to keep track of my expenses, but many travelers recommend the Trail Wallet app for smart phones. Use it to create a budget and keep track of expenses.

**voyagetravelapps.com/trail-wallet/**

Before leaving home, categorize your expected expenses. Here are the expense categories that I use:

- Lodging
- Food
- Prepared Food
- Transportation
- Personal Care
- Tips
- Admissions
- Excursions/Guides
- Technology
- Home Expenses
- Misc.
- Gifts
- Theme Related*

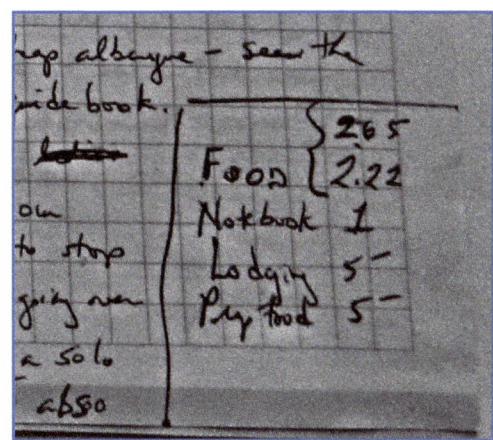

*I keep track of my expenses by category in my journal and record them on a spreadsheet when it is convenient.*

Notice I separate "Food" and "Prepared Food." "Food" is that which I purchase to prepare myself—usually in grocery stores or markets. "Prepared Food" is what I purchase in cafés, restaurants, or food trucks, and includes coffee or tea or other drinks that I buy in a café. If I drank alcoholic beverages regularly, I would separate those out as well, because alcohol can dig a hole in your budget very fast.

* More about Thematic Travel in Chapter 12.

| | Date | Lodging | Food | Food Prepared | Trans-portation | Personal Care | Gifts | Tips | Fiber Related | Admissions | Excursions | Gear/Computers, | Misc. | $ | |
|---|---|---|---|---|---|---|---|---|---|---|---|---|---|---|---|
| 1 | Wednesday | 1-Nov | 10.00 | 2.20 | 14.50 | | | | | | | | | 26.70 | Azura |
| 2 | Thursday | 2-Nov | 10.00 | 9.11 | 8.30 | | | | | | | | 1.00 | 28.41 | Pedrouzo |
| 3 | Friday | 3-Nov | 13.00 | 2.90 | 1.3 | | | | | | | | 23.60 | 40.80 | Santiago |
| 4 | Saturday | 4-Nov | 10 | 10.79 | 2.6 | | | | | | | | 2.00 | 25.39 | |
| 5 | Sunday | 5-Nov | 12 | | 11.20 | | | | | | | | 57.38 | 80.58 | Negreina |
| 6 | Monday | 6-Nov | 6.00 | 1.40 | 6.00 | | | | | | | | 0.85 | 14.25 | Santa Marina |
| 7 | Tuesday | 7-Nov | 12.00 | | 6.00 | | | | | | | | | 18.00 | Dumbria |
| 8 | Wednesday | 8-Nov | 12.00 | 7.03 | | | | | | | | | 3.00 | 22.03 | Muxia |
| 9 | Thursday | 9-Nov | 12.00 | 5.62 | 9.50 | | | | | | | | | 27.12 | |
| 10 | Friday | 10-Nov | 12.00 | 3.34 | 2.00 | | | | | | | | | 17.34 | |
| 11 | Saturday | 11-Nov | 12.00 | 3.09 | 1.70 | | | | | | | | 0.75 | 17.54 | |
| 12 | Sunday | 12-Nov | 12.00 | | | | | | | | | | | 12.00 | |
| 13 | Monday | 13-Nov | 12.00 | | 11.50 | | | | | | | | | 23.50 | |
| 14 | Tuesday | 14-Nov | 13.00 | 4.15 | 10.00 | 8.00 | | | | | | | 20.60 | 55.75 | Santiago |
| 15 | Wednesday | 15-Nov | 8.00 | 3.31 | | 38.80 | | | | | | 11.96 | 20.00 | 82.07 | Porto |
| 16 | Thursday | 16-Nov | 10.00 | 5.00 | 7.00 San | | | | | | | | | 22.00 | |
| 17 | Friday | 17-Nov | 11.00 | | 13.00 | | | | | | 7.20 | | | 31.20 | Alijo |
| 18 | Saturday | 18-Nov | 11.00 | 6.93 | | 11.10 | | | | | | | | 29.03 | |
| 19 | Sunday | 19-Nov | 11.00 | | 2.60 | | | | | | | | | 13.60 | |
| 20 | Monday | 20-Nov | 11.00 | | 14.20 | | 5.60 | | | | | | | 30.80 | |
| 21 | Tuesday | 21-Nov | 11.00 | | 6.00 | | | | | | 1.50 | | 11.00 | 29.50 | |
| 22 | Wednesday | 22-Nov | 11.00 | 12.72 | 2.00 | | | | | | | | | 25.72 | |
| 23 | Thursday | 23-Nov | 11.00 | | 1.30 | | | | | | | | | 12.30 | |
| 24 | Friday | 24-Nov | 11.00 | | | | | | | | | | | 11.00 | |
| 25 | Saturday | 25-Nov | 11.00 | 8.25 | 12.60 | | | | | | | | | 31.85 | |
| 26 | Sunday | 26-Nov | 11.00 | | | | | | | | | | | 11.00 | |
| 27 | Monday | 27-Nov | 11.00 | | | | | | | | | | | 11.00 | |
| 28 | Tuesday | 28-Nov | 11.00 | 11.22 | 2.50 | | | | | | | | 0.65 | 25.37 | |
| 29 | Wednesday | 29-Nov | 11.00 | 8.00 | 16.00 | 4.70 | | | | | 5.00 | | 8.00 | 52.70 | |
| 30 | Thursday | 30-Nov | 11.00 | | | | | | | | | | | 11.00 | |
| | Totals This Month | | 330.00 | 105.06 | 161.80 | 62.60 | 5.60 | 0.00 | 0.00 | 0.00 | 13.70 | 0.00 | 11.96 | 148.83 | € 839.55 | $1,015.86 USD |

*Sample page from my travel expenses spreadsheet*

Travel Expenses Spreadsheet Template

You can download an editable template of my spreadsheet and instructions at: CATHLEENSODYSSEY.COM/dpt-downloads

## SAVING ON LODGING

Of course, everyone has their own minimum requirements for comfort, and expectations vary. When you begin your trip, you many decide that you only want to stay in private rooms. But I do encourage you to try hostel life at least a couple times. It is not just for 20-something backpackers anymore. You are no longer required to do a volunteer job before leaving in the morning (as was the case 40 years ago). Most hostels in Europe are clean and very safe. In some other countries, you have to be a little more discerning. But that is easy now because booking sites are filled with customer reviews that give you a realistic idea of a hostel's suitability for your requirements. If you are using a booking site, like AirBnb or Booking.com and you see a place you like with great reviews, google the name and see if they have their own website. You may be able to book cheaper through their website, or by calling them directly. But sometimes it is cheaper to use the booking site.

If you are staying a week or longer, always ask if the guest-house has a weekly or monthly discount.

If you are visiting a destination in order to see a specific attraction, try to find lodging within walking distance or an easy bus-ride

## A Penny Saved...

away. On my way to Liverpool, I knew I wanted to take a day to visit England's National Coal Mining Museum. A little research showed me that from Manchester it was an easy hour's bus ride straight to the door of the museum. I reserved a bed at the Manchester Youth Hostel for two nights just so I could spend a day at that museum. Only locals use the bus, so I enjoyed several conversations on the way.

*Hostel life...is not just for 20-something backpackers anymore.*

Read more tips for saving money on lodging in Chapter 6.

### SAVING ON TRANSPORTATION

Use public transportation as much as you can. Your cheapest option for getting around is by local bus, tram, tuk-tuk, or combi. When researching your destination, be sure to learn a little about the local transportation system. WIKITRAVEL.COM and ROMETORIO.COM are excellent starting places. On page 40 you can see an example of how I use RometoRio.com to make my way by bus in a new city.

Getting on a local bus can be a intimidating, especially when it is crammed full of people. This can be one of those "I gotta' get out of my comfort zone" moments. If it makes you nervous, reading about my experience of getting on my first local bus in Arequipa, Peru might help. CATHLEENSODYSSEY.COM/courage-blog

"Courage" Blog

TIP
*My daughter, Rebecca, says that another perk of taking public transport as you arrive in a country is that from the start you get a glimpse and introduction to the landscape and people. You can start to make yourself comfortable with the culture.*

### *"But I've Gotta' Driver and That's a Start"*

*I often like to walk between a rail/bus station and my lodging. One of the reasons is to become acquainted with the neighborhood. I had planned to do so when I arrived in Hikkaduwa, Sri Lanka, but as the train approached the station, it began to rain cats and dogs and sharks—one of the last monsoons of the season. I was disappointed. The water was warm so I did not care if I got wet. But then I thought about my "stuff" and how hard it would be to dry things out that evening. So, I decided that if I could hire a tuk-tuk at the station for a reasonable amount, I would do so.*

*The first driver to approach me was Sampath who quoted 300 rupees for the two-kilometer ride to the Citadel Villa—less than $2 USD and a bargain in this weather—I thought. It was raining so hard that I could not see anything outside the tuk-tuk and we had to shout to each other to be heard over the din. But it turned out that Sampath knew just about everyone and every place in Hikkaduwa and he was great friends with my hosts. When we arrived at the villa, he opened the gate, shouted to my host to find out which apartment was mine, drove right to the door, and rushed my packs under shelter. We talked a bit more before he left. When he learned that I was interested in local cuisine and shopping at the traditional market, he offered to be my guide and show me how to cook the dishes. Of course, he was expecting to be paid, but his guiding charges were reasonable, and he promised to only charge me the "local rates" for future tuk-tuk rides in town—150 rupees! I had to laugh!*

*I had a driver for the duration of my stay in this seaside town!*

*A few days later, we visited the local Sunday market and his other favorite shops for ingredients. He returned to my kitchen and showed me how to make dried-fish curry and rice, and we enjoyed a nice repast on my patio. In the coming weeks, he took me to a local tea plantation, the Tsunami Museum, and the fort in nearby Galle. He found a great deal on fresh calamari and showed me how to clean it. And, he invited me to his home to meet his sweet family and to eat a feast that his wife prepared.*

*If it had not been pouring rain in Hikkaduwa on the 28th of October 2018, I would have never met this remarkable man or experienced his radiant smile.*

*Sampath, my smiling driver and guide in Hikkaduwa!*

**Taxis**

I must confess that I am a reticent taxis passenger for several reasons:
- I rarely used them in my life before recent travels and never became accustomed to them. As a result, I often walk farther than most people would. (But I do like to walk, and I sometimes discover some fantastic neighborhoods that way!)
- When using a metered taxi service, it is difficult to know how much the fare will be in advance. The driver can usually estimate for you, but in my experience, that estimation is almost always lower than the final fare.
- Taxi scams are reported all over the world. Some cities tolerate them more than others and up-front research will show you when to be aware of them.

Although I don't claim to be an expert, here are some things I have learned in order to tolerate the occasional necessity for a taxi:
- Before my trip, if I have to take a taxi from the station or airport to my lodging, I contact my host in advance and ask what the taxi should cost. Often your host can arrange transportation for you.
- In some places, taxis do not use meters at all, just tell the

driver where you are going and ask what the fare is. Sometimes you can negotiate, but some communities have set fares that are not negotiable.

- When taking a taxi from your lodgings, ask your host to call the taxi. Ask him to verify the cost with the driver when it arrives, with you present.
- Another taxi strategy is to learn to use Uber or similar taxi alternatives. Grab is a similar service I found in South Asia.

**Rail:**

Every rail system in the world seems to be different. But train lovers have a savior. As mentioned in Chapter 2, Mark Smith, also known as "The Man in Seat 61," provides just about all the information you need to start your rail journeys, including many tips for saving on tickets. He tells you when it is prudent to purchase ahead, when it is not necessary, and a host of additional money-saving suggestions. SEAT61.COM

Two valuable things I learned about trains in the UK from the Man in Seat 61 were:

1. "Splitting tickets." When making reservations, enter your origin and destination to see what the fare is. Note the intermediate stations, especially those where you change trains. Then check to see what the cumulative fare is if you buy separate tickets between each of those stations. The savings can be surprising, as the example itinerary between Berwick-upon-Tweed, England and Oban, Scotland below shows.

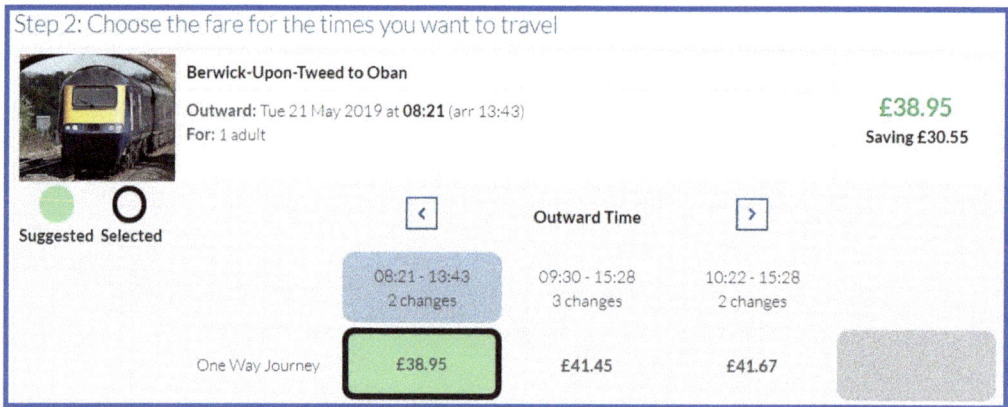

*A Penny Saved...*

*I was planning to be in the UK for about 3 months, so I knew I would save more than enough on discounted train travel to repay the £30 Railcard fee. What a bonus I got when I decided to return to Scotland for a couple more months the following winter. The card was valid for a full year. I was sure glad I had not discarded it!*

2. Discount Railcards. If you qualify and are planning to travel by rail even a few times, a discount Railcard may be worth the £30 cost (£20 for disabled persons). They are available for people who are: 16-30 or over 60 years old, disabled, traveling in pairs, and for families. You don't have to be a citizen to purchase one. It will save you one-third the price on all off-peak travel in Scotland, England, and Wales and it will pay for itself after only a few trips.

You can learn more about saving on rail travel in the UK at:
**RAILCARD.CO.UK/cheap-train-tickets/**

# CHAPTER FIVE

# Food, Glorious Food!

> **In this Chapter...**
> - Frugal Food Strategies
> - Enjoying Local Cuisine
> - Cooking is a Way to Connect with Locals

My strategy for affording to visit some of my favorite countries long-term is to live more like the way I do at home. This especially holds true when I am traveling in Europe, where daily travel costs can mount up quickly. So, I find ways to prepare most of my own meals, saving restaurants, cafés, and street stalls for the occasional special treats or opportunities to sample local fare.

## Frugal Food Strategies

I was in Europe for 13 months during 2017–18. My average monthly cost for all my food, (including food I ate in cafés and restaurants) was less than $300 US (less than $10 per day). Even during my seven days in Copenhagen, food cost me less than $69.00—in one of the most expensive European countries!

In this chapter, I provide suggestions for easy, fast, and healthy meals, and help you develop food-preparation skills to use when traveling. It won't be long before other hostel guests look over at your plate longingly and remark, "Wow that looks good!"

Here are my 10 favorite strategies for saving money on food anywhere I travel.

1. **Choose Lodgings with Guest Kitchens.** Almost all hostels in Europe have guest kitchens. Many guesthouses do as well. Some are quite well-supplied and modern. Most on-line reser-

◄ *Buying oca in Peru. It looks like a fingering potato. It tastes something like a cross between a potato and carrot.*            *Sunday market in Izcuchaca, Peru*

vations systems, like Booking.com will tell you if a listing has a kitchen, and many have photos of the kitchens.

2. **Look for nearby food markets.** Unless I have sleuthed out the nearby markets in advance with Google Maps, one of my first questions when checking in is (after "What is the wifi password?") "Where is the nearest supermarket?"

> TIP
> 
> *Find out when and where the local farmer's market takes place. Shopping there provides unique and fresh ingredients for meals, a chance to save money on your food budget, and an opportunity to experience the local atmosphere, people, and cuisine. Vendors are happy to tell you all about their product and suggest ways to prepare it.*

3. **Check out the kitchen before shopping.** What equipment is there—stove, oven, microwave, decent-sized refrigerator? Is there a time each day that the kitchen is closed for cleaning? Is there a space for you to store your food, both in and outside the refrigerator?

   What staples are already there? You will sometimes find oils, vinegars, sugar, condiments and lots of spices. I often find that I don't need to purchase some of these basic ingredients.

*Many hostels have bright, modern kitchens with several cooking stations, like this one at the Islesburgh Hostel in the Shetland Islands.*

Are there any free food ingredients? Quite frequently there is a "free food" box on a shelf and sometimes even in the refrigerator. Pasta and rice are common. These are items that previous guests did not want to carry away.

4. **Have a shopping plan.** Always make a list and try to stick to it. Think about how long you will be staying in your current location and don't buy too much food. But also, try to purchase enough for your stay or for a few days. If you have to go shopping every evening for dinner, you will be less likely to prepare your own meals.

5. **Develop a travel cooking repertoire that works for you.** Preparing most of your own food means that you have more control over what goes onto your plate. Keep it simple! Develop a repertoire of a few basic and simple dishes that you enjoy eating and that are fast and easy to prepare. Keep it healthy so you can maintain your travel energy. Include lots of fresh vegetables and fruits and very few preservatives, whenever possible.

   It is important that you prepare flavorful foods you like. Then you won't get bored and be tempted to go out. Before you embark on your journey, practice making a few meals as if you were cooking in a hostel kitchen. Even better, eat all or most of your meals this way for a week. Then you can weed out the methods and dishes that don't work for you. When you hit the ground at your first destination, deciding what and how to eat won't be such a difficult decision.

   *It is important that you prepare flavorful foods you like. Then you won't get bored and be tempted to go out.*

6. **Don't get fancy. Stick to the basics.** My goal is to be in and out of the common kitchen as quickly and with as little mess as possible. You can create stunning and healthy whole-meal salads or sandwiches with little-to-no actual standing-over-the-stove cooking, and with very little clean-up.

   Pre-washed greens are very common in European supermarkets—even the small neighborhood markets. Add some favorite fresh vegetables, a hard-boiled egg and flavorful cheese, like sharp cheddar or feta. I often dress salads up with something from my pack like raisins or toasted seeds. Grab a roll from the market bakery or some crackers. If you are really

*Simple, healthy breakfast for travelers on the go.*

hungry, "bake" a potato in the hostel microwave to put on the side.

Sometimes my breakfasts are really quick: oatmeal or muesli, yogurt or milk, fruit, and maybe some seeds.

7. **"Bulk cooking" saves time and money.** A bulk-cooking strategy also ensures you are not tempted to stop at a café after a long day being a tourist.

Don't worry, it is not as hard as it sounds. When I plan to stay in one location for more than a couple days, I will cook up a batch of versatile stir fries, boil a few eggs, cook some rice, and maybe fry up some apples—enough for several meals. During the rest of the week, I will combine these in different ways, so I don't get bored. I may spend an hour or so cooking on the first day, but after that, reheating and laying out the food takes minutes!

For example: Those stir fries are great on the rice the first night. In later dinners, they can be layered cold or hot over a salad, or on a baked potato and topped with feta cheese. Include them in a dinner omelet. Roll up in a wrap for a take-away lunch. Buy an inexpensive instant soup mix in the market and use the stir-fries to dress it up. Your imagination is the limit!

Food, Glorious Food

8. **Pack your lunch.** When you get hungry in the middle of a day out, it is easy to spontaneously purchase expensive prepared foods from a café or street vendor.

   Visiting a museum for the day? Most tourist destinations—like museums and castles—have cafés, but they tend to be pricey. Take a break from the museum to find a nearby park and enjoy that sandwich in your daypack. Have a day of train or air travel coming up? I don't need to tell most of you how bad and expensive airline food is now. How great it will be to have fresh, homemade food with you on the train or flight—better and cheaper—AND you can eat when YOU want to!

   *TIP*

   *Pack your lunch the night before, incorporating leftovers from dinner. I often PLAN to have leftovers just for my next-day's lunch.*

9. **Carry a useful assortment of staples and emergency food.** At any given time, I will have an assortment of some (not all) of the following in my pack:
   - Instant packets of soups/noodles
   - Dried fruit
   - Hard cheese
   - Potatoes
   - Onions
   - Boiled eggs
   - Toasted nuts and seeds (These are very versatile.)
   - Salt

   And I almost always have tea, oat flakes (raw oatmeal) or muesli, raisins, peanut butter, and carrots or an apple. Even if I am too tired to shop when I first arrive at my lodgings, I usually have enough ingredients to prepare a rudimentary supper before I fall into bed.

   *TIP*

   *All of us have our comfort foods. Two of mine happen to be fairly portable—oatmeal (porridge) and potatoes. When putting together your own food bag, consider what your own comfort foods are and brainstorm ways to have at least one of them always available. You never know when you are going to be too tired/sick/depressed/lazy/or whatever to go out—even to the market, and it is nice to have such a simple pleasure easily available.*

Dream. Plan. Travel.

**10. Carry a kitchen "kit."**
- Cup and spoon
- Sealable bowl
- Cloth napkin or bandana
  The above are useful for your packed lunches. The bowl can also be used to store leftovers in the hostel refrigerator.
- Pocket Knife

  I have never encountered a sharp knife in a public kitchen and almost always find myself using my own Swiss army knife.
- Small dry bags *

  I cannot count how many uses these have: shopping bags, lunch bags, or for storing your staples/emergency foods
- Portable immersion water heater *
- Half-liter insulated bottle *
- Zip-lock Bags

Find sources for items in this list which are marked with an asterisk (*) at CATHLEENSODYSSSEY.COM/resources

**Don't get me wrong...**

I love to eat local specialties as much as anyone. In fact, you should see all the foodie photos I have on my Facebook pages! But if you limit the frequency of eating out to only a few times a week instead of three times a day, you will save a great deal of money.

So, eat your main meal in, and go out to that sweet little bakery down the street for dessert. Or grab a pint at the local pub where a band is playing.

Use the coupon code **DreamPlanTravel** for 30% off this e-book when you check out.

All the above tips and much more (including my favorite on-the-go recipes) are covered in detail in my e-book *Food Strategies for Frugal Travelers*. See details about it on page 151 or go to CATHLEENSODYSSEY.COM/bookstore/

Food, Glorious Food

## ENJOYING LOCAL CUISINE

When you do eat in restaurants, try to choose special dishes from the regional cuisine. Before arriving in a new region or country, research the local cuisine to find out:
- the main traditional dishes. Then decide which ones you don't want to miss during your visit. Ask your host where they recommend you will find the best version of any dish.
- the popular street foods and where to find them.
- where the farmers and traditional markets are, the specialties you will find there, and when they are open.
- fresh fruits and vegetables and other ingredients that you have never heard of and how they are used.
- how some of the local foods are made, in case you want to try your own version of them in your guesthouse kitchen.

When you arrive, ask locals what their favorite food is and where to find it. People are proud of their cuisine.

If you are staying in one place for a week or more and if you find a café or restaurant you really like, return a few more times to try different things on their menu. Usually by just your second visit, you will be treated like a special guest. Don't forget to give them a favorable on-line review.

*...ask locals what their favorite local food is...*

*During my six-week stay in Karakol, Kyrgyzstan, I ate about five times at the Alma Ethno Café. Every time I walked in, I got a big smile and a huge amount of delicious local food. And look at the size of that pot of tea! Kyrgyz people don't mess around when it comes to their tea.*

◀ *Fabada:* The ultimate comfort food in Asturias, Spain. I had no idea what it was when I ordered it from a chalkboard, but tears came to my eyes at the first bite!

▲ *Juma:* This strong and healthy concoction of ginger and turmeric is refreshing in the Indonesian heat.

I don't advocate preparing all your own food while traveling, but make eating out a special occasion when you can indulge in the local flavors.

◀ *Cullen Skink:* My friend Emily told me to try this local bisque made of smoked haddock and heavy cream while I was in Scotland. The name may sound a bit strange, but the flavor is extraordinary. Add a pint of dark beer and you have a recipe for pure satisfaction!

▲ One of my most memorable meals in the little town of Santoña, Spain—Verduras de temporada a la brasa con lascas de jamon bellota (*Seasonal vegetables grilled with acorn ham flakes*)

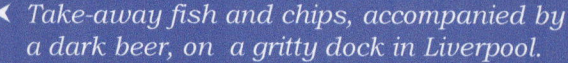

◀ Take-away fish and chips, accompanied by a dark beer, on a gritty dock in Liverpool.

Food, Glorious Food

## COOKING IS A WAY TO CONNECT WITH LOCALS

Once you get to know a few people it is almost certain you will be invited to someone's home to share a feast.

You can find cooking classes almost anywhere in the world and they can be quite a bit of fun. Look for the ones that will take you on a tour of the local market and then teach you how to use the unique ingredients. Ask your host if they know people who would be willing to show you how to cook the local specialties.

Here are some ways I made connections because I showed interest in local food:

- I told my tuk-tuk driver in Sri Lanka that I loved to shop in local markets and learn how to prepare the food. A few days later, he was guiding me through the Sunday market, helping me pick out dried fish, and other ingredients, and returning to my apartment to help me cook it all up.
- I enjoyed watching our host in Krygyzstan as she prepared Ormu, a steamed dough filled with thinly sliced vegetables. I asked if she would be willing to give a cooking class and show us how to make borsook (the local version of fried bread) and before we knew it we had our hands in the dough. You can read about it at:

   **CATHLEENSODYSSEY.COM/making-borsook**

   Making Borsook

- Also in Kyrgyzstan, because I was always asking so many questions, one day my host called me over to show me the samovar. I had heard of this ancient contraption that heats water with a tiny wood fire, but never knew exactly how they worked. I learned that they are still very much in use in Central Asia. You can read about it at:

   **CATHLEENSODYSSEY.COM/samovar**

   Samovar

- In Sri Lanka, I walked into Temptations Café and asked to see a menu. When I wondered aloud what "pittu" was, Raj began to explain. Then he said, "Come back at 4:00 and you can watch me make it." We are still good friends to this day. When I left Sri Lanka, I made a tribute video of Raj. you can see it here: **CATHLEENSODYSSEY.COM/raj-temptations**

   Tribute to Raj

# Chapter Six

# Now I Lay Me Down to Sleep

### In this Chapter...
- Choosing Where to Stay
- Hostels are not Just for 20-Somethings

One secret for enjoying long-term or slow travel is to always try to have a comfortable, safe, relaxing place to call "home." All beds are not equal when traveling.

I have met travelers who rarely planned where they would lay their heads. They arrive in a town and then using their mobile devices, go from place to place just looking for a bed, any bed. I highly recommend making lodging reservations before arriving in a new location. You never know if there may be some event going on and all the inexpensive options are reserved. There was only one time that I did not do so and I was *very* lucky to find a bed because a popular horserace was scheduled in town for the next day. I do not like to walk from place to place with my pack hoping I can find a reasonably-priced bed. If you make reservations in advance, you have an idea of what the lodging is like; you know how much it is going to cost; you know the location; and the hosts are expecting you.

## Choosing Where to Stay

Before you begin looking for lodging, it is important that you know what you are looking for—what will make you comfortable. Do you like to have other people around to socialize with, or do you prefer a quiet location? Do you want a private room or are you willing to share a dorm? How important is a guest kitchen? an

◂ *Albergue de Perigrinos in Güemes along the Camino de Santiago del Norte, Spain.*

*en suite* bath? good wifi? friendly staff? How about privacy, security, or cleanliness? Do you want to be in the city center near all the activity and attractions, or does a small town or rural environment appeal more? If staying in a dorm, is it important to only share with other guests of the same gender?

> *As you travel, experience will help you learn what facilities and amenities you prefer ...*

As you travel, experience will help you learn what facilities and amenities you prefer in a guesthouse or hostel. Here are a few that I check in the on-line listings. If you find a place that sounds great, but you cannot find out if they have a certain amenity, there is usually a "contact the host" option somewhere on the listing and you can ask questions.

- How far is it from places you want to go, including food stores, ATM's, cafés and restaurants, as well as tourism sites that are interesting to you. If you can walk to these places, you will save taxi fares or the need to learn a new bus system.
- How far is it from the airport/station from which you are arriving/departing? Is the lodging easy to get to upon arrival? Some hosts will arrange transportation for you at an additional charge if you ask them. But be careful, there may be cheaper ways to get to the lodging.
- Is breakfast provided? Can other meals be purchased on site—especially if the guesthouse is in an out-of-the-way location?
- Is there a guest kitchen? Preparing and/or storing some of your own food can save a great deal of money. (See Chapter 5 for more about that.)
- Check reviews closely—especially if you are staying more than one or two nights. You want to be comfortable. Is the host/staff hospitable and helpful? Is the place clean? Do they enforce rules regarding guest behavior? (This is especially good to know about hostels.) Is it quiet at night? Is it a party hostel?
- On Booking.com, I usually don't even consider any location that has a review rating of less than 8.0.
- Are there strict check-in/out times? (For example, if you are arriving late, can you still check in?)

*My spacious room in Otavalo, Ecuador. My rent included the use of a nice kitchen, comfortable living room and a rooftop terrace. Is it any wonder I did not want to leave?*

**What about cost—what is your ideal price range?**
One way I decide on how much to pay for my lodging is to take the nightly rate and multiply it by 30. Believe it or not, I want that amount to be less than what I would expect for rent in my home country. During my 13 months in western Europe, my monthly average for lodging was slightly more than $500 per month. I mostly stayed in hostel dorm rooms. During the low seasons, I often had a dorm room to myself just for the price of a bed!

When I moved on to Asia and South America, the cost of lodging plummeted. There I almost always had a private room or apartment (sometimes with my own private kitchen) and my monthly housing costs averaged $391 per month.

If you are staying for a week or longer, be sure to contact the hosts ahead of time to see if they offer a discount. I got a 19% discount on my six-week stay at Aylluwasi, an incredible guesthouse in Ecuador—less than $300 per month!

Many hostels these days provide both private and dorm rooms. When traveling solo, I usually opt for a dorm bed. But a private room sometimes only costs a little more than two dorm beds. So, when traveling with friends you may want to consider a private room.

Keep in mind that your lodging includes utilities and maid service, sometimes breakfast, and almost always free wi-fi. Compare that with your daily living costs at home.

### TIP

*If the location has not yet been reviewed because it is a new listing, the rates may be lower. I once got a great rate for an unrated and unreviewed AirBnb room in Glasgow because when I looked at the listing, it was apparent that the host was very professional. So, I took a chance. As it turned out, she had been renting the room for years to fellow visiting musicians and had a lot of experience hosting guests. But she had just started listing with AirBnb. It was a gamble that paid off. I ended up extending my stay.*

### The Hospitality of Strangers

*As I travel and meet local people, I am amazed at the invitations I receive! The connections I have made through my knitting and spinning have been remarkable. A post in a Lace Knitting Group Facebook page resulted in being invited by Connie in the Netherlands to stay in her home for three days. We only met face to face when she picked me up at the train station and we connected instantly! She and her husband became great friends, and when I (jokingly) suggested that she join me in Estonia in a few weeks, she took me up on it. We spent another week together meeting some very well-known Estonian lace knitters and had a great time!*

*In Utrecht, I met Lili in her yarn store, Sticks and Cups. When I said I was going to Copenhagen, she insisted that I meet her friend Charlotte. I did, and when we picked up our knitting at the same time, we were both knitting socks from the same kind of yarn purchased at Lili's store! I was having difficulty finding weekend lodgings and she offered her spare bed in a lovely apartment overlooking Copenhagen's harbor.*

*While walking the Camino de Santiago, I shared an albergue one night with Caitlin and Gerry from Roscommon, Ireland. We got to talking and when Gerry learned that I liked to "mess around with wool," he invited me to visit them when I came to Ireland and to make plans to come to the annual Roscommon Lamb Festival. I ended up spending 3 weeks in their lovely cottage apartment in January and then being a guest artist at the Lamb Festival the following May!*

Think about these things before you begin perusing booking sites for reservations. Then you can begin your search by using the site's filters to eliminate the types of lodging you don't want.

**Booking Sites**

For hostels, I use Hosteling International (**HIHOSTELS.COM**) or **HOSTELWORLD.COM** to make reservations. For guesthouses, I mostly use **BOOKING.COM**. (A similar site is **AGODA.COM**.) Booking.com usually presents you with locations that have dorm rooms, but you can easily filter them out if you prefer private rooms. Many hostels now offer private rooms as well as dorm rooms. (More about hostels below.)

I used to use **AIRBNB.COM** to search for lodging. I still use it if I am wanting to experience a true homestay with a family. But I am careful in my searches because in the last few years, I have found that AirBnB's system will nickel-and-dime you to poverty. If you are only staying a few days, the cleaning and service fees tacked on by many hosts may double the advertised price. And, you pay a 6% booking fee to AirBnB as well. If you stay a week or more, you can usually get discounts, AND those service fees get spread out over many nights. So, do the math when using AirBnB to see if it is providing you with the best deal.

Find a few booking sites that work well for you and stick with them. As a Booking.com regular I usually get a 15% discount for my bookings through them.

*Find a few booking sites that work well for you and stick with them.*

While I was in the UK, I booked hostels through the Hosteling Scotland and England's Youth Hostel Association and regularly received coupons from them. During the winter low season, I frequently received email coupons for 25% off my stays!

## HOSTELS ARE NOT JUST FOR 20-SOMETHINGS

The only way I can afford to travel in Europe is to find lodging in hostel dorm rooms. I remember the hostels of the 1970s and I cannot recall anyone over about 30 years old sleeping in them. But now, hostels have moved along with the times and the baby boomers. Many have dropped the word "Youth" from their name. Most have private rooms available for couples and families. Yes, most of their clientele are still young people, but I regularly meet other people over 50—especially in the rural and small-town hostels.

Staying in hostels assures company and from fellow travelers, you will learn about even more places to visit. They will encourage you to visit their country. (That is how I ended up in Sri Lanka for three months!) They will offer you a place to stay. (That is how I ended up at the Roscommon Lamb Festival in Ireland!) You will find other people to join on temporary excursions. (That is how I ended up hiking the Triund Trek near Dharamshala, India with two young women from Azerbaijan and India!)

> *Staying in hostels assures company and from fellow travelers, you will learn about even more places to visit.*

By looking for hostels in the Hosteling International network (**HIHostels.com**), you are assured that certain standards are met—

### Hostel Etiquette

- Read and follow posted rules. There is a reason for them.
- Even if quiet hours are not posted, use your common sense and be as quiet as possible between 10:00 pm and 8:00 am.
- Clean up after yourself. Keep your belongings as close to your bed as possible. Use the lockers provided. Don't block access to an upper bunk.
- If you have an early check-out try to pack as much as possible the night before, so you don't awaken your roommates rustling with plastic bags in your pack and talking with traveling companions.
- Use earphones for listening to music or watching videos. (Sounds like common courtesy? I thought so too!)
- Please, put your smelly shoes outside the dorm room. Some hostels have special drying areas for wet clothing. Some hostels require that you leave your walking boots or street shoes in the foyer.
- When preparing food in the kitchen, wash up and wipe counters before you eat so that those following you will have clean utensils and space to work.
- There are usually cubbies for storing your food in the kitchen. Do not "borrow" food from other people's cubbies. (Again—sounds like common courtesy, doesn't it?)

like cleanliness, accessibility, gender-segregated dorms, and enforced guest rules for guests like quiet hours, etc. A small fee gains membership in the network and you usually receive a discount off non-member prices. "Independent" hostels (those outside the Hosteling International network) may also be clean, quiet, comfortable and safe, but when reserving one, you should read about the facilities, the rules, and reviews a little more carefully.

The hostel staff can be very helpful in orienting you to the local environment and activities. They understand that you are traveling on a budget and often offer economical tours of their own. In rural areas, they seem to know all the hiking and biking trails. Some hostels will host barbeques, movie nights or other special events. And tables in the dining room are oriented to encourage people to eat together and visit. One hostel I visited even had a "no mobile devices during breakfast" rule.

Dorms have lockers available to secure your belongings. Bring your own lock, or you can rent one from the front desk.

TIP

*Ask hostel staff or owners to recommend hostels for your upcoming destinations. I have stayed in some very charming places as a result of such inquiries.*

## The Cons of Hostel Life

There are some disadvantages to staying in hostels, so take note:
- You have a lack of privacy especially if you are staying in a dorm room. Although I *have* stayed in a couple of hostels which sported curtains across the front of the beds.

TIP

*I usually travel with a shawl or light blanket. If you sleep in a lower bunk, you can usually tuck the fabric somewhere in the bed above you to create a curtain to provide privacy and block the light.*

- Most hostels offer gender-specific dorms, but some do not. You can check on that when you make your reservation. If you walk in without reservations, you may only have a mixed dorm to choose from.
- Bathrooms are shared and sometimes they are down the hall. In a few hostels, both men and women share the bathrooms.

- Almost all dorm rooms have bunk beds.

*TIP*

*If you prefer a lower or upper bunk, email the staff in advance to state your preference. Almost every time I have requested a lower bunk in advance, I have gotten one.*

- People snore (and make other noises during the night). If this is unacceptable, bring earplugs. As a woman, I try to reserve a room in a female-only dorm, mainly because there tends to be fewer people who snore. (Sorry, guys!)
- If there is no curfew in the hostel, noise at night can be a problem. Check reviews in advance to see if anyone warns about this. It can especially be a problem in city hostels.
- Some hostels require that you vacate the dorms and other areas during the day so the staff can clean. I was usually able to just move to a common area if I was not planning to go out that day. But you should always ask if this is okay—the staff appreciates that. If the kitchen has "closed for cleaning" hours posted, abide by them.
- Sometimes you have to make your own bed and strip it when you check out.
- A bath towel is not always included. I always have my own towel. You can usually rent one for about $2.00 or so.
- During school holidays or weekends there may be school or youth groups in the hostels, creating a little more noise than usual. The times that I have encountered these, the chaperones have done a reasonably good job of keeping the children quiet. They are assigned their own sleeping quarters, so you don't have to worry that you will be sleeping with a "slumber party" crowd.

**Develop a List of Hostel Requirements**

On my last trip, I stayed in over 90 different hostels, in dorm rooms—mostly in Europe. No wonder I am so comfortable in them. They are all pretty much run the same way—some much better than others. Below is my list of requirements (in order of importance) when I look for a hostel. On the booking site, I research the facilities list, photographs, and reviews to decide which locations meet my requirements. As you gain experience, you will come up with your own list.

- Affordable—I try to stay below 25 Euros for a dorm bed in Europe, but they can be much less during low season and depending on the country.
- Not a "party" hostel!
- Clean
- A kitchen—preferably with a microwave, stove, teapot. A toaster is nice.

### The Black Sheep Hostel

*Sometimes you find a hostel that just seems to have it all. The Black Sheep Hostel in Killarney, Ireland fit the bill for me! Host Blaine Lyne, raised in Killarney and very proud of his community, was the epitome of friendliness and helpfulness. He marked a local map with all the best hiking trails in the nearby national park, and told me the advantages of each one.*

*A well-stocked grocery store was less than two blocks away. Breakfast was provided. We were welcome to use the daily harvest of fresh eggs from the hostel's flock of chickens. It was wintertime and there was a nice fire in the living-room hearth most evenings.*

*Bicycles were available for rent; movie nights were arranged every Tuesday; and traditional Irish stew was served on Sunday night.*

*When Blaine found out that I was on the lookout for knitters, he arranged for me to meet his mother—also an avid knitter.*

*Our room had a bath en suite; sturdy privacy curtains fronted each bed; large lockable drawers were conveniently located under the bunk; each guest had their own electrical outlets, shelf, and reading light; and there was plenty of headroom between bunks.*

*Cost per night? Less than 18 Euros.*

▲ Happy Nomads Yurt Camp in Kyrgyzstan was a paradise of flowers. The cosy felt yurts muffled all sound and ensured a good night's rest. The included breakfasts were among the best I ate on my trip.

▲ Bodenaya was probably my favorite of all the albergues I experienced while walking the Camino de Santiago in Spain. David provided a serene environment and served up an amazing dinner and breakfast AND he washed our sweaty clothes for us while we slept. The cost? "Donativo" (a donation)

▲ Islesburgh Hostel in the Shetland Islands was situated in an old mansion. The brilliant dining room was so welcoming, I did not want to leave. Indeed, I stayed there for eleven days!

▲ I was welcomed at Albergue Playa de Poo with a cup of tea in their outdoor dining room. Breakfast included fresh eggs from their chickens. Nearby was an unusual estuary beach.

▲ Howmore Hostel in the Outer Hebrides was set in a traditional thatched "blackhouse" with 13-inch thick stone walls. It was one of the quietest places I have ever slept.

- Helpful, friendly staff
- Convenient location for the activities I have planned
- Good wi-fi
- Near a decently-stocked food market (not convenience store)
- Fairly quiet between 10 pm and 8 am
- Good showers with hot water (not on-and-off hot water)

The following are nice to have, but not deal-breakers for me:
- Convenient electrical outlets near the beds
- Comfortable open common area and dining room
- Separate male and female bathrooms. When bathrooms are *en suite*, that is a real bonus. (All bathrooms are separated by gender in Hosteling International hostels.)
- Plenty of space between the beds in the dorm rooms and enough headroom between the bottom and top bunks so that you can sit easily. Check the photos.

Keep in mind that hostels have to work on a strict budget in order to pass on the savings in the form of inexpensive lodging to you. This means that the front desk may not always be open; rules are stricter than in a hotel; short-term volunteer staff may not know all the ends-and-outs of the hostel's operation.

No matter what kind of lodging I am looking for, during my research, I spend plenty of time perusing the reviews, photos, and facility listings. If I will only reside a night or two, I am not so picky about the facilities, but the longer I plan to stay, the more careful I am to make sure it is a good fit for my requirements. I browse the photos and read reviews carefully. As you have seen, location, cleanliness, a quiet location, and staff friendliness are high on my preference list. I balance cost with comfort and have sometimes ended up in some very special places.

You can find a list of my favorite hostels and guesthouses in the Appendix.

> *I balance cost with comfort and have sometimes ended up in some very special places.*

# CHAPTER SEVEN

# Taking Care of Business

**In this Chapter...**
- Your Personal Assistant at Home
- Other "Business" Considerations
- Working on The Road
- Keeping in Touch

There are many aspects to a long-term trip to consider that you don't have to think about when you are absent from home for less than a month. It is fairly easy to find a friend to watch your house, water plants, etc. for a short time. But you probably don't want to leave your house empty, your mail uncollected, or your mortgage and other bills unpaid if you will be absent long-term.

Even though I do not have property to consider, I began thinking about these kinds of things about eight months before I embarked on my recent trip.

Here are a few things to consider:
- Management of your house or apartment. Will you have renters, subletters, house-sitters? Will you close it up and have a trusted friend check on its condition occasionally? How will things be managed if something goes wrong in the house or apartment? Will you turn it over to a property manager? Are there pets to consider? a garden?
- Management of your "stuff." If you are renting or subletting your residence, you probably have to find storage for some or all of the items you own.
- Automobiles. They should not be left undriven for long periods of time. Do you want to loan it out? have someone use it occasionally? sell it? Do you need to continue to pay for car insurance? What are the penalties in your state if the registration lapses?

◂ *One of my many "offices." This one overlooks Dharamkot, Himachal Pradish, India.*

- Health insurance. It is unlikely that your health insurance will cover you while you are out of your country. You will need travel insurance for that. (More about that later.) But, if you have to return home after several months because of a health problem, will your insurance still be valid? In the US some insurance companies have minimum annual state residency requirements, for example.

*...if you have to return home after several months because of a health problem, will your insurance still be valid?*

In this chapter, you will also find suggestions about paying bills and other financial matters, working on the road, and keeping in touch with friends and family.

### TIP
*I found it useful to start a "Getting Ready to Leave" notebook to make sure I did not overlook any important details of these types. Create a header for each item of business that needs to be taken care of before leaving. Start making checklists, taking notes, and finally scratching off the completed tasks. If you are comfortable using electronic note-taking apps, like Onenote or EverNote, you may like to use one of those instead.*

### Your Personal Assistant at Home

Early in your planning, find a friend or relative whom you trust and is willing to take care of your "home" business. This may end up being several different people, depending on what kinds of business you want them to handle. Here are some things your assistant(s) can do for you:
- Receive boxes you send home and send items to you.
- Make deposits to your bank accounts when you receive hard-copy checks.
- Have access to your storage unit if you have one.
- Be an emergency contact.
- Take care of mail collection.

Make sure someone at home is a joint account holder and has signature access to your bank account(s). Leave them some hard-copy checks. If something happens to you, they will be able to send money from your account to anyone you specify with ease.

Leave copies of the following with someone you trust:
- passport information page
- travelers' insurance documents
- will
- advance directive
- personal instructions in case you are incapacitated

## OTHER "BUSINESS" CONSIDERATIONS

- Mail collection and management. Try to sign up for paperless communication for as many accounts and services as possible. Then you will receive critical alerts and messages via email while you travel. You can appoint a personal assistant at home to take care of physical mail.
- Paying bills. Go through all the recurring bills: mortgages, rent, storage spaces, insurance, loan payments, etc. Make sure they are automatically paid or that you receive them by email when they are due. Then make sure you know how to pay them online. Don't forget those quarterly and annual bills.
- Bank and credit card accounts. Sign up for online banking and make sure you know how to use the account interface to transfer funds.
- Set up any recurring payments so they are automatically deposited to your bank account and not sent to you as a check in the mail.
(Of course, you may already do these things even when are not traveling.)
- Contact bank and credit card companies and set up travel notices on your debit and credit cards so your cards won't be blocked when you try to use them outside the country. If you deviate from your itinerary, be sure to update the travel notices.
- Set up a Virtual Private Network (VPN) for working securely online. If you are using wifi in public areas, like cafés and hostels, it is possible for others to see what you are doing

*...set up travel notices on your debit and credit cards so your cards won't be blocked when you try to use them...*

online, including learning user names, passwords, and credit card information. If you set up a VPN, your logins will be invisible to possible attackers.

There are other advantages to using a VPN. Some websites, including most financial institutions, will not allow you to log in from a foreign network. With a VPN, it appears to the site that you are physically located in your country. Many travelers also use a VPN to be able to stream movies from their Netflix account. I use **ExpressVPN.com**.

- For trip plans that include driving internationally, you may need an International Driving Permit (IDP). Google "international driving permit (name of your home country)" to find out how to order one. It is also a good idea to familiarize yourself with local driving laws and road signs and symbols beforehand.
- Pack copies of all trip-related documents: passport ID page, visas, driver's license, credit cards, Medicare card, etc. If you store them digitally, be sure they are password protected and that you can access them even if you don't have access to wifi.
- Purchase traveler's insurance. Make sure that it will cover not only trip cancellations and your baggage, but, more importantly, your medical care in case you are injured or become ill. Most travel insurance companies also provide a free concierge service to help you find non-emergency medical/

*"Working on the Sea!" My overnight ferry from Copenhagen to Tallin had excellent wifi, so I took advantage by getting some work done in my little cabin.*

dental care and other types of assistance. Don't leave home without it because your regular health insurance plan is not likely to cover you once you cross the border.

## WORKING ON THE ROAD

These days there are lots of opportunities for using your skills to earn enough money to travel long term. The Internet has leveled the playing field.

If you already work in the high-tech field, you may be able to convert your current office job to a remote occupation. More and more employers are accepting this from their employees. Do some research on the Internet. Brainstorm ways that you could do your current job, or a closely related one, remotely. Create a formal presentation for your boss, and just ask. You might be surprised.

Travel bloggers GoatsOnTheRoad have published an informative post about working remotely. It includes a section on how to pitch your remote working idea to your existing employer.

GOATSONTHEROAD.COM/remote-work/

If continuing to work for your present company doesn't work, keep brainstorming. Google "working while traveling" for lots of ideas.

> *I have done a couple kinds of work remotely. I sometimes take on graphic design jobs creating book layouts and brochures for clients. I was even working on a hiking book for a client while walking the Camino de Santiago in Spain! Every week or so, I took a couple days off from walking, found a hostel with good wifi, and got to work. I also worked as a virtual administrative assistant for an estate executor. My clients usually pay me with hard checks sent to my personal assistant who deposited them for me.*

## Keeping in Touch

Because of almost universal Internet availability, it is easy to stay in contact with friends or even conduct business back home. Whether you are calling your credit card company to replace a lost card, or just connecting with a friend because you cannot wait to tell them about a recent experience, phone calls using mobile phone, tablet, or laptop are easy and virtually free.

*... your friends are anxious to hear about your adventures.*

Many of your friends are also anxious to hear about your adventures, so it is a good idea to set up some way to share stories and photos easily.

### Calling Family, Friends, and Businesses

**Cell Phone:** I have managed all my foreign travel without a cell phone—mostly because I did not want to figure out how a new cell phone company worked every time I moved to another country. It is challenging to anticipate what the cost will be. Of course, that means I do not have any Internet service when I am away from wifi.

All that being said, many travelers I encountered do use cell phone service while in other countries. Some sign up for international service with their home company, but this can be expensive. If you have an unlocked GSM smartphone, you can remove your home service's SIM card upon arrival in a new country and replace it with one from a local company. Most travel bloggers say that the best place to negotiate for mobile service is at the airport. Another option is to purchase an inexpensive pre-paid phone abroad. If you want mobile coverage while traveling, research all these options to decide which is best for you based on how you expect to use your phone.

**On-line Phone Apps:** The two phone apps I use are Skype and Facebook Messenger. Other popular phone-and-text apps include WhatsApp and Google Hangouts. Whatsapp seems to be a current favorite throughout the world.

Choose a couple apps and get used to how they work. I found that sometimes I had a poor Skype connection, but Facebook Chat was clear. Not all of them will allow you to call landlines or mobile phones, so choose at least one that will. Some friends and

> **Skype**
>
> Skype is one application that allows you to set up a subscription to make unlimited calls to landlines and mobile phones in countries of your choice for a nominal fee. That way your contacts do not need to have a Skype account in order for you to call them. For a modest monthly or quarterly amount, you can sign up for "Skype to Phone" and be able to call phones anywhere in specific countries for free. (For example, for less than $3.00/month, I can call anywhere in the US or Canada and talk as long as I want to. When I was in the UK for several months, I signed up for "Skype to Phone" in the UK as well.)
>
> You can also put some Skype credit on your account so you can make quick phone calls to any places outside those specific area—usually for about eleven cents per minute. Ten dollars in your account is plenty to make occasional short calls outside your specified "Skype to Phone" country.
>
> You can also set up a Skype number that people who don't use a phone app can use to call you.
>
> The disadvantage of using Skype is that you have to have Internet access to use it.

most businesses will not use phone apps, so you need to be able to call their mobile phones or landlines.

## Sharing Your Adventures

**Email lists:** One simple way to send travel updates to people is to create an email list. Then periodically, you can send messages with photos and stories to the list. As interest in your travels grows, it is easy to add people to the list. Be sure to use the BCC: (Blind Courtesy Copy) option instead of the TO: or CC: field for email addresses. This way, you keep everyone's addresses private, and recipients cannot use the REPLY TO ALL option.

**Using Facebook:** I also use my Facebook page to write what I call "mini posts." They are faster and simpler to compose than a blog post, so I am able to send short updates out more frequently. However, my audience is limited to Facebook users who check their feeds regularly.

My friend Nev created a Facebook mini-blog. He set up a Facebook page separate from his personal page and gave it a name representative of his travels—Roads to Roam. Each day he wrote a journal entry with photos of the day's travels. You have no control of photo placement, but it is a simple solution for those who are acquainted with how to use Facebook. And, you don't have to learn how to use a blog app.

At present, if you mark all your posts "Public," friends who are not Facebook users can access your posts. However, the screen is shorter and Facebook keeps bugging the reader to log in or create an account. And they will have to make the effort to check the page regularly. There is a work-around. Create a mailing list of those friends who request regular updates to your travels, but who are not Facebook users. Then you can email them links to each public post. Here is how you copy the links:

⇒ Once the Facebook post is published. Make sure the Privacy Setting for the post is "Public." If it is, there will be a tiny globe next to the date/time stamp.

⇒ **If you are on a mobile device**, touch and hold on the date and time stamp at the top of the post. A window will pop up with the link of the post at the top and options. Tap "Copy link address." Then you can paste the address in an email or a text message to anyone, including people who don't use Facebook.

Taking Care of Business

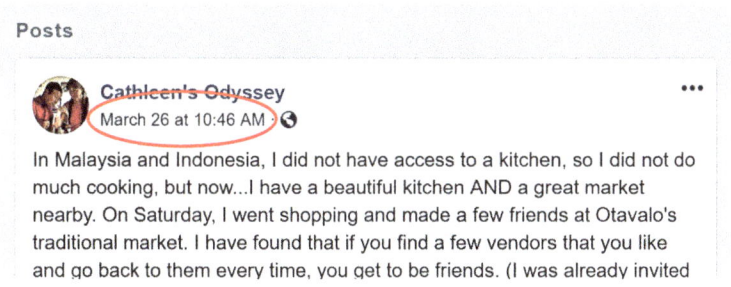

⇒ **If you are on a computer**, right-click the date and time stamp at the top of the post. An options window will pop up. Choose "Copy link address." Then you can paste the address in an email or a text message to anyone, including people who don't use Facebook.

> *Right before I left on my first trip to Peru, my friend Myra, said, "You're going to write a blog about your trip, aren't you?"*
>
> *"No," was my immediate answer. But it was not long before I realized that creating a simple blog was an easy way to keep friends up to date on my travels.*

**Blogging:** I have talked to a lot of travelers who say they use a simple blog to keep friends and family informed and share their experiences. It does not have to be complicated. If you are just starting out blogging, I recommend Google Blogger—but only if you are pretty sure you are not going to one day try to expand and make a full-fledged professional travel blog. In that case, bite the bullet and learn to use Wordpress. Wordpress is much more complicated to learn to use than Blogger, but it is more powerful. When I started my blog in 2013, I had no desire to become a professional blogger. But five years later, I changed my mind and it was a LOT of work to convert it to a more appropriate format.

### TIP
*If you decide to author a travel blog, even if you do not plan to earn money from it, I recommend reading "How to Start A Travel Blog" at Nomadasaurus.com.*
**WWW.NOMADASAURUS.COM/how-to-start-a-travel-blog/**

# Chapter Eight

# STUFF (OR, WHAT I PACK)

**IN THIS CHAPTER...**

- Think Small
- Packing Strategies
- My Portable Office
- Useful Items I Don't Leave Behind

The items I carry around the world vary depending on where I am traveling and what I am doing there. When I was in Europe, I was exploring knitting and spinning with locals. So, I brought along my tools of the trade and was intentionally purchasing yarn and raw fiber frequently. My pack would slowly fill with fiber until I had enough to justify sending it home. When I moved to Asia, where there were fewer knitters, I did not accumulate these souvenirs and traveled more lightly.

In this chapter, I don't really give you a packing list. You can google for that online and find lots of suggestions. This is more of a packing strategy. You want your baggage to stay as light as possible without leaving essentials at home. When initially deciding what to bring along lay out everything and sort it all by priority. You may end up eliminating most of the low-priority items. Do several test packings during the last week before your trip so you have plenty of time to make decisions about what to eliminate. Remember that you can purchase many items while on the trip.

*Do several test packings during the last week before your trip so you have plenty of time to make decisions about what to eliminate.*

◄ *My three traveling companions: backpack, daypack, and waist bag. The little bear was a gift from a Scottish hostel and he gets a front seat hanging from my waist bag.*

Dream. Plan. Travel.

> ## WHY I DON'T USE ROLLING LUGGAGE
>
> - You need a smooth surface. In many places you will be walking on cobblestones, dirt roads with mud puddles, and uneven sidewalks.
> - They are challenging to use on a crowded sidewalk.
> - The wheels add several pounds to the load, and you will be carrying it often over the uneven ground mentioned above.
> - A backpack serves double-duty—You can use it for overnight treks and city-to-city travel.
>
> Get the smallest backpack you can get away with. It will force you to limit what you carry, and thus you will have less weight to lug around.
>
> ### TIP
> *Before checking a backpack for a flight, be sure all the straps are tied down and secured so they don't get damaged.*

## THINK SMALL

Advantages of having a small backpack:
- You really must limit the items you carry!
- You are not tempted to buy souvenirs. Sometimes, when I am just admiring local craftwork, and the vendor is bugging me to buy, I am able to say, "I don't have room, I only have a small pack." I doubt it makes them feel better, but I do like having an excuse, and sometimes they leave me alone to look.
- It will be lighter, and when you have to walk (sometimes several kilometers) with all your stuff, you will be happy about that!
- When you don't have items in your pack that require being checked into the luggage hold, if your pack is small enough you can carry it on, saving baggage fees.

# Stuff

### TIP
*Train before your trip. It will not be unusual to have to walk up to a kilometer carrying/rolling all your belongings. Be sure you can do so. If you are deciding whether to take a backpack or rolling luggage, do a test. Load up your pack or rolling luggage with the weight you are expecting it to have on the trip. Do the same with any smaller bags/daypacks/purses you will be carrying. Find about two blocks of sidewalk that needs quite a bit of repairing. See how easy it is to roll/carry all the bags up and back. Envision yourself doing this many times on your trip. Then decide what kinds of luggage you will take.*

## PACKING STRATEGIES

- Sometimes you will land in a city and only have to stay one night there before moving on to your final destination. You only need a few things for that one night. Put all those items in your carry-on daypack. That way you don't even have to open your pack and you are ready for a quick departure the next day. (If any of those overnight items must go into your checked bag—like liquids over 100 ml—put them in the very top, or in a side pocket, of the larger backpack.)

*I liked the fact that my Deuter backpack has a zipper in the bottom of the main compartment so much that I installed a zipper in the bottom of my daypack as well. This has come in handy so many times. I can put my raincoat or a sweater there (out of the way from things on top), but if it rains or gets cold, I can retrieve them quickly.*

Dream. Plan. Travel.

- When moving between a hot climate to a cool one (like from sweltering Indonesia to the cool mountains of Ecuador), pack clothes appropriate for your destination in the top of your large backpack. Then you can change clothes in the destination airport before you go outside.
- I partly roll and partly stuff my clothing. I roll larger things like pants and shirts. I keep out small items, like underwear, socks, and my rayon skirt, and stuff them in the empty spaces between hard items.
- Be sure to have a rain cover for your backpack. You will use it! My Deuter pack comes with an attached raincover that stores in the bottom of the pack.
- I have never used packing cubes, but many travelers really like them. It seems to me that they would work better in traditional luggage than in a backpack. I do use various sizes and colors of drawstring bags for sorting small items.
- When packing your daypack, try to visualize which items you will need most often during the trip and put them on top.

### TIP
*Get a pack with a unique color (Mine is turquoise.) You will locate it quickly in the bus hold or as it comes off the airport carrousel. (And you won't accidentally pick up someone else's black bag that looks just like yours.)*

## MY PORTABLE "OFFICE"

I don't travel with an actual purse. I choose utility over style and my "purse" is actually a waist bag that I have used for many years when traveling. I jokingly refer to it as my "office," and I usually keep it strapped around my waist and in front of me for easy reach of most things I need. I can also carry it over my shoulder. This is great for solo travelers because you can keep often-accessed items

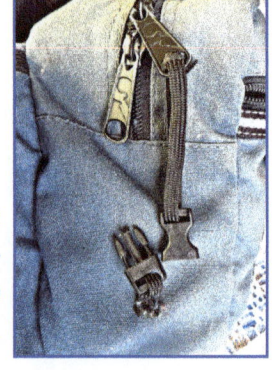

*To make it more difficult for pick-pockets to access the main compartment of my waist bag, I installed a small quick-release clip on one zipper pull so that I can fasten it down to the side of the pack. I use it when walking in crowds of people.*

*Stuff*

handy when you don't have someone available to search your daypack.

I use the Outdoor Products H2O Mojave waist bag that has holders for two 500 ml water bottles. My 50 ml Healthy Human insulated bottle fits perfectly in one holder. Sometimes I temporarily slip my camera in the other bottle holder for quick access while walking around. (Be careful about doing so in crowds of people.) The pack is quite spacious and I often add my travel journal, a snack, mini tripod, knitting project, or small purchases. A poncho or rain jacket can be strapped to the outside.

Here are some of the things I keep close at hand in my waist bag.

- Auxiliary battery pack and USB cable
- Camera and extra batteries
- Tablet
- Wallet/Money belt
- Water bottle
- Tissues
- Lip balm
- Notepad and pens

## Useful Items I Don't Leave Behind

Here are some things that I almost always pack. You can find sources for items marked with an asterisk (*) in the Cathleen's Odyssey Resource page. CATHLEENSODYSSEY.COM/resources

Cathleen's Odyssey Resources

1. **Auxiliary battery pack*** to charge my mobile devices when I don't have access to electricity.
2. **Head lamp or flashlight**
3. **Quick-dry clothing**—especially pants
4. A **wrap-around skirt or sarong** comes in handy and not just for clothing. Opened up, my skirt is over a meter wide and when I am sleeping in a dorm room, I can hang it from the bunk above me to create a privacy curtain. It is quick to don in the middle of the night when I make a trip through a public hallway to the bathroom. The skirt I have can also convert to a sundress.

Dream. Plan. Travel.

5. **First aid kit** (See Chapter 9.)

6. A **lightweight blanket or shawl** that packs down small is useful when traveling on air-conditioned vehicles and airplanes. Bundled up, it can be a make-shift pillow. It can also be hung from an upper bunk bed to create a privacy curtain.

7. **Universal sink stopper.** The sinks in many hostels and guesthouses do not have stoppers. Carrying one with you means it is quick and easy to wash out a few clothes.

8. **Draw-string sorting bags*** to keep things sorted and to use for packed lunches and shopping.

9. **Small dry bags*** Use these water-proof bags: as shopping bags; as a food bag for traveling; store damp clothes when traveling to your next stop; to keep electronics dry on a rainy day. Stuff one with clothes to make a pillow. You can even wash your clothes in them.

10. A **foldable bag/pack*** that does not take up much room can be useful for the long-term traveler who occasionally has to transport more things than will fit in the main pack. If you are going on a multi-day excursion and want to store some belongings at your guesthouse while you are gone, you can use this bag.

11. A **Swiss army knife** is useful for lots of things. But for those who use guesthouse kitchens, it is essential. In two years of travel I have yet to find a sharp knife in a public kitchen.

12. A **portable immersion water heater*** means you can prepare hot drinks and instant soups and cereals, even when you have no kitchen.

13. An **insulated bottle*** for carrying hot drinks on the go.

14. A **spoon, sealable bowl, and plastic cup** rounds out your tiny portable kitchen.

15. A **bandana** has so many uses, I cannot list them all here, but I don't do without one.

16. **Trekking poles** help you keep your balance when walking on rough roads and terrain, especially if you are carrying a load on your back. They are also useful for waving away unwanted dogs. If you have a clamp-on mini-tripod, you can easily convert your trekking pole into a selfie-stick.

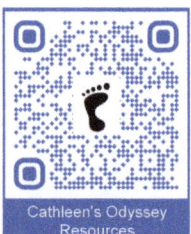

* You can find sources for items marked with an asterisk in the Cathleen's Odyssey Resource page. CathleensOdyssey.com/resources

*Stuff*

17. **Duct tape.** Don't leave home without it. You will find a use for it…I promise!

18. A **luggage lock and cable\*** mean you can secure your pack when it is stored at the end of the train car in places that are prone to theft. In hostels, you are sometimes required to supply your own lock for storage lockers. Having your own will save the rental cost.

19. An **assortment of clips.** You will often use binder clips, **carabiners\***, clothespins, safety pins, paper clips, etc. to hang items from your pack and connect things together.

20. **Elastic shock cord\*** can also help you connect things to your pack. If you make giant rubber bands from it, it will hold items together inside your pack. It also helps to have a few heavy duty rubber bands.

21. About 20 feet/6 meters of **paracord** or rope.

22. **Small dispenser bottles\*** are great for taking small amounts of creams when the containers they come in are large.

23. Heavy duty **zip-lock bags** in assorted sizes.

24. **Mini sewing kit** which includes heavy-duty thread and needles. You will have several opportunities to make repairs to clothing and equipment.

25. **Universal Power Adapter\*** If you travel with any electronics, you will use one of these. I like the kind that have at least a couple USB ports so I can charge my laptop and other devices at the same time. (Be aware: this is not a *power converter*. It will not convert power from 220 to 110 volts. But your computer and other devices should have converters built in to their power cord.)

26. I don't use my **USB Flash Drive** often, but when I need it, I am glad to have this tiny item.

27. I always have my own **towel.** Many hostels either don't provide bath towels or they charge a fee for them. Some guesthouses near beaches don't allow you to take their towels to the beach.

28. My **RoadID bracelet\*** is not actually packed. I always have it on my wrist. It provides lots of information to emergency personnel in case I am incapacitated—even if my passport or other ID is nowhere near me. You can read more about RoadID on page 123, or go to CathleensOdyssey.com/road-id

# Chapter Nine

# OFF THE BEATEN TOURIST PATH

**IN THIS CHAPTER...**

- Finding the Nooks and Crannies
- Low-Season Travel

The two main ways I am able to avoid crowds and touristy sites is to look for the nooks and crannies and embrace low-season travel.

## FINDING THE NOOKS AND CRANNIES

If you are traveling "slowly" and staying in one place for a while, you have the opportunity to ask your host and other locals to suggest unusual and rarely-visited sites. I always ask about places to walk in the countryside, where I usually encounter even more locals who have suggestions. You won't find out about these places in guidebooks.

### Off-the-Beaten-Path Rewards

*There was not a tourist in sight as I walked along the Urabamba River in Peru's Sacred Valley. I encountered a farmer who was having problems balancing a load of cuy (guinea pig) fodder on his cart. I offered to hold it for him as he pushed the cart back to his village. We walked along talking and laughing. When we arrived in the tiny hamlet, he stopped at his door and called to his wife so she could meet me. They invited me in for muña (a kind of mint) tea and he proudly showed me his livestock: three huge bulls and a couple rooms full of guinea pigs, which they raise for food. As I left, he invited me to the village Easter festival coming up in a couple weeks!*

◄ *Miles from nowhere...Along the trail to Choquequirao, Peru*

Dream. Plan. Travel.

In a city, exploring nooks and crannies means merely walking a few blocks away from the hoards of tourists. Taking my time, I peer into shops and bakeries that sell no trinkets or gifts, but just the everyday goods that locals need. I look UP at the apartment balconies above the shops and wonder who lives there. Sometimes I wave a "hello" up to someone. Since it is usually apparent that I am not a native, people will often stop and ask where I am from and we get to have a conversation—more or less, depending on the language challenges. Asking them to suggest a good place to eat shows that I respect their local knowledge, and even more conversation can ensue.

*...people will often stop and ask where I am from and we get to have a conversation*

In the country and villages, it takes even less effort. Choosing to lodge in an out-of-the-way village means you can easily walk through the countryside watching people at work in the fields and frequently strike up a conversation. Also, almost everyone knows who lives there so it is readily apparent that you are an outsider. And because they know (and are probably related to) many locals, they can make very reliable recommendations about what to see and what to eat.

*Walking a few blocks off the main streets in Porto, Portugal, I came upon a huge cemetery next to a cathedral. It was like a miniature walled city with family mausoleums for buildings and tiny gardens sprinkled throughout. A bit of fog was moving in giving the scene some mystery. I was enchanted and spent over an hour exploring.*

## Off the Beaten Tourist Track

> **TIP**
> *When it is apparent that you are a tourist in a village, or even a city neighborhood, you can walk down the street and most likely, very few locals will greet you. BUT, if you greet them first with a "Good morning" in the local language, they will almost always return the greeting and often stop to chat.*

Staying in some kind of homestay, using a booking site like AirBnb or Couchsurfing, is practically guaranteed to provide you with many opportunities to travel like a local. It is not unusual for your host to show you around the neighborhood and introduce you to friends and family. Many people love to share their cuisine so don't be surprised to find yourself in their kitchen cooking up something you have never heard of.

> *While staying in Belfast, Northern Ireland, my host gave me a personal tour of the city's "peace lines" that were erected during the late 20th Century "troubles" and still exist today. She had worked with youth on both sides of the line during the 1990s and was very familiar with the neighborhood and those who still live there.*

### LOW-SEASON TRAVEL

"Low season" means different things depending on your destination. Some destinations have several high seasons in one year. Hawaii is one example. It has a high season in summer and again during each of the US school vacations. In most temperate climates, the high season is summer, low season in winter, with a couple shoulder-seasons in spring and fall. In South Asia, high season is governed by the local monsoons. For example, in Sri Lanka, high season on the west coast was November through March; on the east coast it is May through September. However, when you are close to the equator, the temperatures are fairly constant all year round. For countries with very hot summers, you may want to consider visiting in the winter.

My main reason for enjoying low-season travel is the lack of crowds and other tourists. You have more chance of having a seat to yourself on the train. Servers in restaurants have time to give you better service. It is easy to find affordable lodging.

Dream. Plan. Travel.

## The Wild Atlantic

*The January night after I arrived on Inis Mor, one of Ireland's Aran Islands, a storm hit with brutal 90-mile-per-hour winds. I sat cozily in the wee pub next to my hostel. Cozy is an understatement! The fireplace was still decorated for Christmas and radiated warmth and good cheer. Only one local stood at the bar watching the football game, so the bartender had time to sit, chat, and knit with me. The next morning the winds were still howling. The local guides had no business because the ferries were not running. There were only three other guests in my hostel and we arranged for one of the guides to take us around the island. He regaled us with history and stories as he drove, but about all I recall now are the stops at the beaches where we were mesmerized by the Atlantic Ocean gone wild. The horizon was just a line of watery mountain peaks.*

*Later while chatting with a shopkeeper and looking from her window at the view of the port below, I was told that in summer there are so many people in the streets that you cannot even see the ferry dock—3000 or more tourists per day on an island of 800 inhabitants! But on this cold, but clear day, she had plenty of time to visit with me and tell me the places I should not miss while on the island. I stayed ten days.*

*This knitting shop clerk had plenty of time to sit and knit with me for a while on a cold winter day.*

> *I was in Copenhagen in July—high tourist season. All accommodations are more expensive and often difficult to find on summer weekends. As one weekend approached, I could not find a bed for less than about $50 US—quite a bit outside my budget. I considered spending the weekend across the country, but still could not find affordable lodging. It was a good lesson on planning which seasons to travel. Yes, Denmark would be pretty cold in the winter, but spring or fall would have been a better time to visit for easy-to-find affordable accommodations.*

**Why I Embrace Low-Season Travel**
- People tend to be more welcoming. During hectic high seasons, locals sometimes get understandably frustrated with all the crowds they have to put up with. But when things slow down, they relax and will be more likely to engage you in conversation, invite you to coffee, and more.
- Everything is cheaper—flights, accommodation, and food.
- Lines to the most popular sites are short or non-existent. People working there have more time to chat with you.
- It is much, much easier to find accommodations.
- If you are staying in dorm rooms, you will often have the whole room to yourself. At worst, the rooms usually won't be full, and you won't feel so cramped for space.
- There is more time for introspection and journaling. Winter can be an excellent time for a personal or guided retreat.
- Yes, the weather may be cold or rainy, but take some time to observe the effects of clouds, fog, rain, or snow, and see how beautiful the landscape can become. Autumn leaves and spring flowers are something summer visitors never experience.

> *I discovered the joys of low-season travel in 2018, when I decided to spend the winter in Ireland and Scotland. Since the theme of my travels at the time was to meet other knitters and spinners, I figured that since those were "indoor sports" of a sort, it would not matter if the weather was inconducive for normal tourist activities. So I braced myself for the cold and proceeded north from Portugal in December 2017.*

### *The Women of Patabamba*

In 2015, I was on a solo day hike in the Sacred Valley, climbing up, up, up to the ruins of Huchy Qosco. I encountered a local guide coming down the trail as I was trudging my way up. While he waited for the couple he was guiding, he struck up a conversation asking all the usual questions, "Where are you from? Do you like Peru?" etc. Then he asked, "Esta solita? Donde esta su guia?" (Are you alone? Where is your guide?), as he looked around behind me. He could not fathom a tourist climbing up to Huchy Qosco without one.

A bit later, I encountered a horseman leading his packhorses down. He also stopped to talk. During the conversation, I told him that I was in Peru to meet other women who spin and knit. He said that his wife, sister, aunt, mother-in-law all could spin and knit, and that I should come to his village to meet them. As it turned out, he was developing his property in the village of Patabamba into a cultural tourism homestay. He asked if I would like to visit. He said that he was also a taxi driver and could transport me to the village. So I took his phone number and said I would think about it. We both continued on our way.

A few days later, I met him at the road that went up, up, up for 45 minutes to his little village. The women were welcoming. It soon became apparent that they had had some cultural tourism training and that I was to be a guinea pig. Adjacent to their home, construction of the guest rooms had commenced, and I was taken on a tour. There would even be toilets and running water. They had killed a lamb over the weekend and the carcass hung on the wall of their home. One leg was to go into the soup for my lunch. And, in fact I helped peel potatoes and cut up carrots for the soup. A young woman and a grandmother accompanied me out to the top of the cliff overlooking the Sacred Valley and we sat companionably together knitting and spinning. After lunch, I spent several more hours exploring spinning, backstrap weaving, and admiring the handmade goods they had for sale. One young girl, about ten years old, was fascinated with my camera, so I handed it to her so she could take photos herself. They turned out to be some of the best images of my trip.

As the sun set, and the day grew cooler, I found myself hoping that my host knew that I planned to return home the same day and NOT stay overnight. Eventually he came around and arranged for another driver to take me down to the bus stop.

I will never forget this incredible, unplanned excursion that gave me the opportunity to experience a cultural tourism site in its infancy and to help in its development.

*Two of the Patabamba women and one little woman peeking around her mother.*

**Low-season Challenges**
- Many tourist attractions are closed or have limited hours. It is important to do your research if you plan to visit specific sights to make sure when they will be open.
- The weather will be uncooperative. Find a favorite weather-forecasting site and make plans around the expected weather. If the next few days are going to be miserably cold, plan to visit a museum or work on an indoor project or take a class. When a day or two is expected to be clear, plan a hike or walking tour. The day may still be cold, but you can bundle up. Plan to duck indoors in the middle of the day and enjoy a hot drink and some warmth.
- In South Asia, the monsoons characterize the low season. Be prepared to get wet. Carry an umbrella. Make sure you have covers/protection for anything you are carrying. The rain will be warm and not terribly uncomfortable if you accept it.

TIP

*"Shoulder season"—usually spring and fall—is a good compromise for most temperate climates.*

# Chapter Ten

# Staying Well and Safe

**In this Chapter...**
- Before You Leave Home
- Practice Healthy Habits
- Learn How to Make Water Safe To Drink
- First Aid Kit
- If You Get Sick
- Safety
- Insurance

In two years of travel, I was very lucky and had no real mishaps and only a few colds. But I was prepared in several ways, not the least of which was my attitude. I decided from the beginning that if I was not enjoying the trip, I would go home. And, I found some kind of balance between worrying too much about what could go wrong with being prepared in case it did. You can read ways that I keep myself safe and *feeling* safe on pages 16–18.

In this chapter I will give you some pointers on more things you can do to travel safely and keep well.

## Before You Leave Home

Research the Center for Disease Control (CDC) website for health-related information about the countries you're visiting. (This is a US government website, but it has health-related information that is relevant no matter where your home country is.)
**www.cdc.gov**

Visit your doctor for additional advice and any required vaccinations or medications. Schedule the appointment for 4–6 weeks before you leave in case you need to take a series of vaccines. Ask your doctor for recommendations in case you get hit with food poisoning, traveler's diarrhea, or have a bad infection.

◂ *One of many incredible hikes I experienced during my two-year journey. Aran Island, Scotland*

If you are going to an area where outbreaks of malaria, yellow fever, or similar diseases are prevalent, discuss strategies for preventing or alleviating them. (Some countries require that you have a yellow-fever vaccination certificate if you have previously traveled to an area where there has been an outbreak.) Be sure your tetanus and other vaccinations are up to date.

Get a supply of your regular prescription meds to hold you for a while. Carry them in their original, clearly-labeled containers and keep a written copy of the prescriptions in case you are stopped in customs. You can get more medications while traveling, but it might mean a trip to a local clinic first. A letter from your doctor describing your condition and listing the prescribed medications (including generic names) will be helpful if you need to visit a foreign clinic. Double check to be sure your medications are not illegal (even if you are carrying a prescription) in the country you are traveling to. If they are you may need to talk to your physician about alternatives.

*A letter from your doctor describing your condition and listing the prescribed medications will be helpful.*

If you are going on a long-term trip, a visit to the dentist is a good idea as well.

Okay, now for the tough recommendation. Get in shape. You will be walking quite a bit, even if you don't have actual hikes or treks planned. You know the drill, start out easy—walk no more than is comfortable each day. Then begin increasing your distance until you can easily walk three miles. At some point in your training, gradually add weight until you can carry all your packs and bags for at least a mile. If you do have a trek planned, you need to train even more.

### Practice Healthy Habits

- Yogurt or probiotics and oats daily can keep your digestive system working smoothly.
- In each new country you visit, ease into the new diet. Before I began my travels, my physician told me that many times, when travelers have digestive problems, it may not be food poisoning. Our guts are just not used to the different strains of good bacteria that reside in various parts of the world. Eat-

## Staying Well and Safe

ing yogurt or taking probiotic capsules can help the transition. I have never had a bad case of food poisoning when traveling. But I do occasionally experience a day of nausea or minor diarrhea or vomiting. If it happens to you, take it easy for a day, drink plenty of fluids, and eat bland things like bread or oatmeal. Don't let yourself get dehydrated.

- Drink plenty of clean water. Most guesthouses provide filtered water to refill your bottles. More and more towns all over the world have stores with a filtered water tap where you can refill bottles as well. I always carry water-purification tablets, but I have rarely had to use them.
- Get exercise and fresh air. When traveling, this can be easy—just keep walking.
- Wash your hands frequently and use sterilizing hand gels only as a backup.
- Use sunscreen.

## Learn How to Make Water Safe to Drink

Ask your host if the tap water is safe to drink. Often they will have a water filter that you can use to refill your bottle. Be aware that sometimes locals can drink the water with no problems, but it may make you sick.

I prefer not to purchase bottled water because of the plastic waste. If my host does not provide filtered water in a location where tap water is unsafe, here are the ways I treat it, in order of preference.

1. A portable ultraviolet light water purifier made by Steripen. It will purify one liter of water in 90 seconds. The battery needs to be recharged periodically, so I carry a backup method, like chlorine or iodine tablets (see below). You can find a source for a Steripen on the Cathleen's Odyssey Resource page.
   **CathleensOdyssey.com/resources**

Cathleen's Odyssey Resources

2. Often grocery stores and restaurants will refill your bottle for a modest sum (usually around 30 cents US). In northern India I found a station with free filtered water on the street that was maintained by a local Buddhist community.

   **RefillMyBottle.com** is an app that will help you locate water refill stations around the world.

3. If you have access to a stove, boil water for one minute and let it cool.

4. Chemical disinfectants using chlorine or iodine can be purchased in camping stores. They add a bad taste to the water that is ameliorated somewhat by letting your bottle sit open for an hour or so. Constant use of these chemicals is not good for you, but they take up little space, so I always keep some on hand in case no alternative is available.

## First Aid Kit

I made an appointment with my pharmacist before my first trip abroad and she spent quite a bit of time helping me decide which meds and first aid items might be useful. You don't need to take too many things, unless you are traveling to very remote regions. You will find pharmacies all over the world. Indeed, in some developing countries there seem be several per block.

Here is what I took with me or gathered along the way:
- A collection of bandages, gauze pads and tape
- Steri-strips™
- Alcohol skin prep pads
- Moleskin to prevent blisters
- Hydrocortizone cream
- Antiseptic cream or ointment
- Antifungal cream
- Anti-itch cream
- Water-purification tablets
- Cough drops
- Pain relievers: ibuprophen (which also serves as an anti-inflamatory) and acetomenephen
- Anti-diarrhea medication
- Antihistimine (for allergic reactions and travel sickness)
- Benadryl (antihistamine) which is the same drug as Dramamine (for travel-sickness) so it serves two purposes
- (Be sure to record recommended dosages on any medications so there is no doubt when it comes time to use them.)

I also had scissors, tweezers, and sewing needles (for splinters), elsewhere in my pack.

Staying Well and Safe

> **TIP**
> 
> *Generic names for some medications differ from country to country. For example, acetaminophen (as it is called in the US) is known as paracetamol almost everywhere else. Brand names are almost always different depending on the country. If you need to purchase medications over the counter, look up the generic name for it and write it down because pronunciations differ depending on the language. The pharmacist should be able to look up the local name for the medication if she has the generic name.*
> 
> *Another option is to use Google translate to learn the name of the item you plan to purchase before visiting the pharmacy. Download an image of the item to your mobile device. Then you can show the pharmacist what you need.*

> *When I was in Sri Lanka, I used Google Translate to find the name for ibuprophen in Sinhala script and then showed that to the pharmacist.*

## IF YOU GET SICK

- Don't hesitate to find a clinic if you don't get well after a few days. Ask at the local tourist office for recommendations or use your traveler's insurance concierge service to locate a clinic for you. They usually can find a clinic where English is spoken.
- Keep drinking fluids.
- Lay low. Change plans. Don't try to continue your normal routine. Give your body a chance to heal.
- If you have severe dehydration, persistent vomiting, bloody stools or a high fever, or if your symptoms last for more than a few days, seek medical help.

## SAFETY

New travelers, especially solo travelers, can sometimes get caught up worrying about safety to the point that it is difficult to enjoy the journey. It is certainly a good idea to take precautions and be aware of local scams and safety issues, but don't allow fear to overwhelm you. Read again, the section "Aren't You Afraid?" in Chapter 1.

Keep in mind that most places in the world (outside warzones) are as safe or maybe even safer than your home country. The safety precautions you take at home will serve you well anywhere you travel.

**Research:** Learn about how safe your destination is. Your government's travel website can provide information on safety and any travel alerts or known scams. Being aware of problem areas or activities will make you more vigilant. Many of the suggestions I make in Chapters 3 and 4 regarding planning and preparations will mean that you are familiar with your destination in advance.

**Arrival:** Try to schedule your arrival to a new place for daylight hours. This provides not only safety on its own, but you will feel safer. If this is not practical, consider arranging personal transportation to your lodgings ahead of time. Then you will have a driver meeting you inside the terminal or airport.

**Using ATMs:** If you know ahead of time how much to withdraw, you will (1) be sure you have enough money in your account, and (2) not be trying to figure out the local exchange rate while standing in front of the ATM. When using an ATM, it is best to look like you know exactly what you are doing and get in and out as quickly as possible.

If you have to withdraw a large amount of cash, try to do so at an ATM at a bank with a security guard at the door. If that is not possible avoid a crowded location. But you also don't want the area to be empty of people, either. As soon as practical, move most of the cash to a money belt or other secure place. Carry in your personal bag or wallet only what you need for the day.

**Neighborhood safety:** If you are concerned about street safety, ask your host or the local tourist office how safe the area is. Some places may be perfectly okay to walk during the day but a bit sketchy at night.

If you do end up in an area where you don't feel secure, walk with assurance, like you belong there. Research your route ahead of time so you are not constantly looking at a map. If you need directions, go inside a shop and ask.

The more you travel, the more confident you will become about judging where it is okay to walk alone and where it isn't.

Staying Well and Safe

*One of many options for personal identification that can be found at* CATHLEENSODYSSEY.COM/road-id

**Identification:** Carry clear identification on you at all times. Check out the ID bracelet and information service offered by RoadID. I keep a RoadID bracelet on me 24 hours a day. The company provides a personal web page about you that paramedics and/or other aid officials can access if you are unable to communicate. On the web page, you can list medical conditions, emergency contacts, passport information or any other information that may be pertinent in an emergency. My RoadID bracelet provides peace of mind, especially when I am swimming or taking part in an activity where I don't have my regular ID with me.
WWW.CATHLEENSODYSSEY.COM/road-id

**Solo Excursions:** If you are going out alone for the day—especially if you are going to a remote area, leave a note with your host or at the front desk telling them where you are going and when to expect you back. Be sure to check in when you return.

TIP
*Carry the business card or address of your lodging with you. That way, if you get completely lost, you can show it to a taxi driver and easily return.*

**Traveler Registration:** Check to see if your country has a traveler's registration program. For example, if you are a US Citizen, you can register with the State Department's Smart Traveler Enrollment Program (STEP). You will receive emails if there are any travel alerts at your destination. I usually find these alerts to be overly cautious sometimes, but I am glad to have the service available to me in case there is a true emergency situation. The STEP program also makes it easier for family to contact you through the embassy if there is an emergency at home.
STEP.STATE.GOV

## INSURANCE

*If you can't afford travel insurance,
then you can't afford to travel.*

Once you are outside your home country, it is not likely that your home health insurance will cover you. Most medical insurance policies are invalid once you step across the border. So, the solution is to always have travel insurance of some kind. It will provide you with the peace of mind that your medical expenses or emergency evacuation will be covered. On top of that, most travel insurance companies offer trip cancellation and delay coverage, baggage coverage, and even concierge service. Need a doctor or dentist right away? Call them and they will find one for you!

*Most medical insurance policies are invalid once you step across the border.*

> *Knock on wood...I have never had to make a claim on my insurance, but they have been helpful a number of times when I needed to find a doctor or dentist in a strange city.*

Another thing to consider is this: if you have to return home after several months (or years) because of a health problem, will your medical insurance still be valid? In the US some insurances have minimum annual state residency requirements, for example. Check on this before you leave home.

I have never had to use my traveler's insurance, thank goodness. Over two years, I spent a bit more than $1,700 for my World Nomads insurance, but it was worth it to have the peace of mind anytime I started to see things going awry. I got pretty sick a couple times and wondered if I would end up going home. I had a horrible cold in Malaysia that was on the brink of pneumonia before I finally sought out a clinic. Although I was pretty miserably sick, I did not have to worry about affording care if I ended up in the hospital. It turned out that my office visits were so inexpensive that I did not bother to claim them.

Take plenty of time to shop around for an insurance policy that is right for you. Some companies will not insure you if you

## Staying Well and Safe

are over a certain age or if you will be traveling for more than 30 days. An excellent resource for researching insurance is TRAVELINSURANCEREVIEW.NET

Leave a copy of your insurance policy and proof of insurance with your emergency contacts. If your embassy or emergency personnel contact them, it will be very helpful for them to have the policy information available. Your emergency contacts can also contact the insurance company to get advice on your behalf if they have the policy details in hand.

### Sick as a Dog in Malaysia

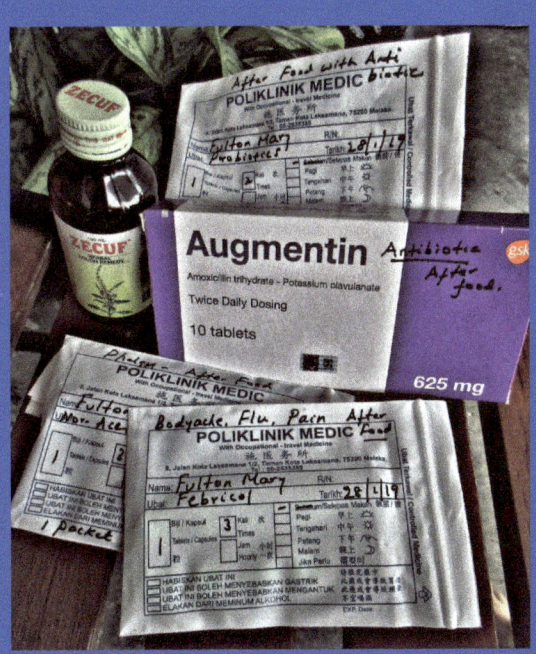

After languishing with a bad cold, the worst cough of my life, and a sinus infection for four days in Malaysia, I finally decided to go see a doctor. My guesthouse host recommended a clinic just across the street. There was no wait. In about 15 minutes, the doctor prescribed antibiotics and probiotics, some kind of expectorant, a pain reliever, and herbal cough medicine. They provided it all right there—no need to go the pharmacy and wait. Total cost? $26 USD! (The office visit was only $7.30 USD.) I did not bother to send a claim to my travel insurance. I was just sorry I had waited so long to seek help.

And I got a bonus: the doctor's wife, Grace, invited me for lunch at her house when I got to feeling better. And we are now Facebook friends!

# CHAPTER ELEVEN

# Mental Health

**IN THIS CHAPTER...**
- Preventing Burnout
- Practicing Gratitude
- When Things Go Wrong

When traveling long-term, you will experience days when you feel down, homesick, stressed out. After all, this is real life and you most likely experience these feelings occasionally at home too.

## Preventing Burnout

- Don't try to pack too many activities in a short amount of time. Don't try to move too often to a new destination. Slow travel is the answer.
- Do things YOU enjoy. Don't think that you are obligated to visit the local castle because that is what everyone does. If you have had your fill of castles on this trip, then don't go. Ask yourself what you really want to do.
- Stay creative. What drives you creatively? Art? Writing? Designing? Music? Cooking? Photography? Don't stop doing those things just because you are traveling. In fact, you will enjoy your trip more if you find ways to integrate your passions, talents, and skills into your travel lifestyle. See "Thematic Travel" in Chapter 12.
- Keep up a healthy lifestyle. Eat well; drink plenty of water; stay active. See "Practice Healthy Habits" in Chapter 10.
- Be a mindful traveler. See "Mindful Travel" in Chapter 12.

◀ *On the beach at Tintagel, Cornwall, England.*

If you do get the "blas" or feel depressed:
- Ask yourself if it is time to slow down. Take a day (or several days) off from traveling. Find some introspective or creative things to do. OR, just veg on Netflix for a day.
- Call a "cheerleader." Friends and family are excited to hear from you. Telling them your stories will remind you what an incredible adventure you are on. Relating your woes will encourage them to help you get over the hump. They may have helpful ideas that you have not thought of.
- Ask yourself "If I could do anything I wanted to right this minute, what would it be?" Don't feel guilty if it turns out that you just want to veg all day.
- Make a list of all the great experiences you have had on the trip so far—especially the unexpected ones.
- Go for a walk in a quiet place. Enjoy the fresh air. Research has shown that regular walking is an excellent antidote to depression.
- Use journaling to figure out what is making you depressed or blocking your ability to enjoy your trip.

*"If I could do anything I wanted to right this minute, what would it be?"*

> *In Indonesia, I was totally blocked. I did not want to work, walk on the beach, go snorkeling...nothing. I wasted several days not accomplishing much at all. Then I decided to just start writing about how I truly felt in my journal. It was not long before the answer appeared on the page. I discovered that because I did not have specific plans and reservations for my next destination, I was being stymied because of the indecision. I spent a few hours planning my routes and making reservations to fly to Quito the following month. After that, I was able to concentrate on my work, which, at the time, was writing this book!*

- Familiar food can be the cure. Ask any long-term traveler what he will eat as soon as he arrives home and you will most likely get a quick and confident answer. (Mine is a juicy homemade American hamburger!) What foods are you missing? Can you find it or make it where you are? You may be surprised how comfortable it makes you feel.

*Sometimes, a café con leche, a bite to eat, and unlimited time to regurgitate my feelings on paper is all it takes to alleviate the "blas."*

Remember: You can go home whenever you want to. Homesick? Just tired of traveling? Not what you thought it would be like? There is no shame in calling it quits.

## PRACTICING GRATITUDE

*From my travel journal:*
*"Many nights I went to bed just*
*exclaiming to myself 'I am in Peru!'"*

One facet of Mindful Travel\* is to practice gratitude. When you travel extensively, there is a great deal of hustle-bustle and stress in planning, keeping track of schedules and possessions, being in strange places, coping with culture shock and language differences, and trying to stay healthy. It is easy to lose touch with how wonderful the experience is.

This is where a regular practice of gratitude can turn an everyday travel experience into something amazing. It does not matter how you conduct your practice—through prayers, meditations, reflection, journaling, simple awareness, or whatever works for you.

\* More about Mindful Travel in the next chapter.

### Finding Gratitude in Disappointment

*Sometimes (well, many times) when you are traveling, things don't turn out the way you envisioned them. I had such great plans to visit some parts of Scotland: the Isle of Skye, the West Highland Way, Eilean Donan castle, the Jacobite Steam Train.*

*THEN...life happened...it was the rainiest July in many years in the UK. Rain and wind everywhere. AND...I had forgotten to consider that July/August is holiday time in Europe and the UK. It was about impossible to find any kind of affordable accommodation on Skye. Also, I learned that the West Highland way is a veritable highway in the summer.*

*Instead, I chose a few days to tackle part of the Rob Roy Way and set off.*

*In two days I got drenched and dried off six times. There were no great Highland vistas—just clouds, mist, fog, and the slosh of my wet shoes. Near the end of the second day, I reached into my pack and found that the pants I had planned to wear to sleep in were DAMP! It would be a cold night. I happened to be at a crossroads, There was a bus stop and a bus was coming in 40 minutes. I was really NOT having fun, and I asked myself, "What is the point of this?" I bailed on the hike and tried not to cry.*

*The next day, I made plans to move on to England after six weeks in Scotland. I felt let down. I wrote in my journal:*

> *I did not see the Isle of Skye, Castle Eilean Donan, the Knockando Woolen Mill, knitters on North Ronaldsay.*

*But then I made a list of all the special experiences and encounters. Here are a few of them:*

1. *Collecting hintelagets and spinning them on Bressay Island*
5. *Knitting with the women in Haddington*
7. *Camping alone by the Falls of Leny*
9. *Managing at midnight in Kirkwall without a room*
10. *Cream Tea at Victoria's Vintage Tea Room in Unst*
14. *Walking on the beach at North Ronaldsay—seals!*
18. *Eating Cullen Skink*
19. *Meeting Antje at the Yarn Cake*
21. *Riding REAL trains*
22. *Photographing puffins*
24. *Sleeping near the Arctic Circle at the summer solstice and listening to birds singing all "night"*

*Okay, I was discouraged about not doing four things, but I ended up listing 24 AMAZING things that I did experience.*

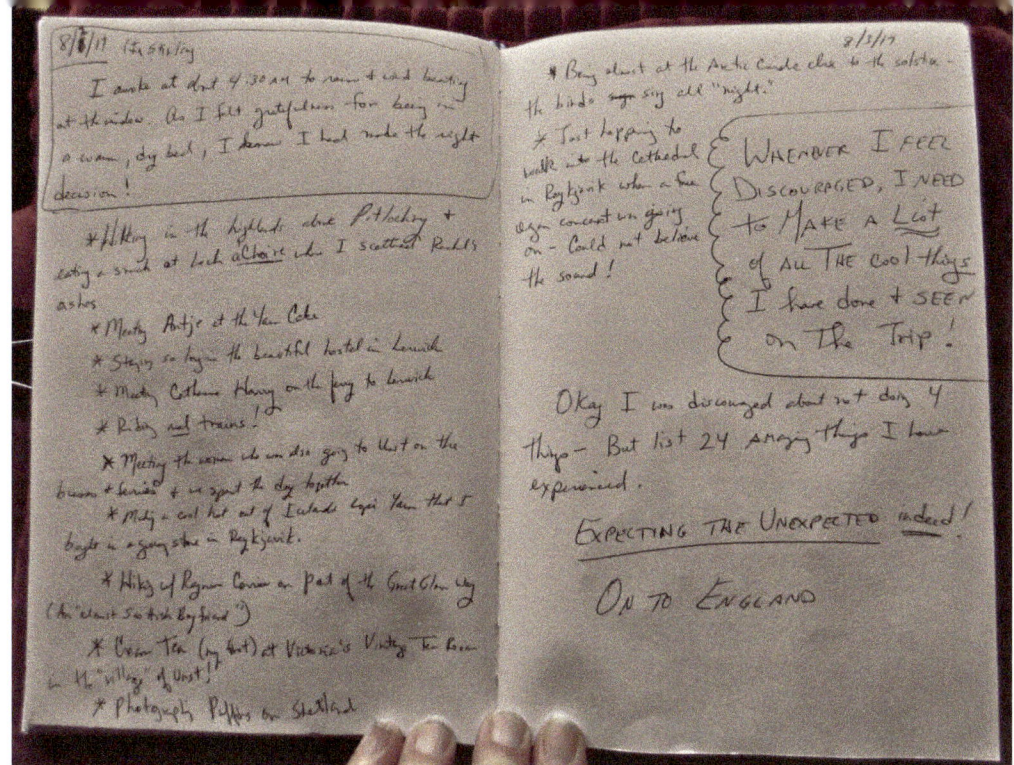

*A few of the 24 wonderful experiences I had in Scotland.*

If you find something every day to be thankful for, you may be amazed at the almost magical results. You become more and more aware of how many things there are for which you are grateful. Soon, even the difficulties become subjects for gratefulness. For example, yes, I was disappointed when it was pouring rain when I arrived in Hikkaduwa, Sri Lanka. I was looking forward to walking to my lodging. But now, I would have to take a taxi. But if that had not happened, I would never have met Sampath, who became a great friend. (See the story on page 64.) Gratefulness in difficulties allow us to learn the lesson that is imposed upon us—that is, to take each and every moment as it comes to us and appreciate it as it is. Before long, when something goes wrong, you automatically look for which facets of the problem you can be thankful for. Then you appreciate the situation for the experience and lesson it is providing.

### TIP
*When learning to practice gratitude, make a list of specific things for which you are grateful. It can become an ongoing list that you keep adding to. Each morning, choose one item and reflect on it during the day. Writing in a journal about it enhances the process.*

Dream. Plan. Travel.

### *A Couple Near-Misses*

*The only ferry to Orkney Island lands near Kirkwall at midnight. I thought I had reservations in a guesthouse, but when I arrived in the wee hours, I found a tiny deserted reception room. There was a phone and number to call. When the sleepy owner answered, she had no idea of who I was. She tried to be helpful, but all her rooms were full, and she could not think of a solution for me. I told her I had a tent and asked if there was someplace I could pitch it. She suggested the campground "on the other side of the Tesco's." (Where in the world was the Tesco's???) Luckily, I had downloaded a Google map of the town in advance and it showed me where I was and identified the Tesco supermarket. Not too far to walk, but it IS disconcerting to walk around a strange town at night with packs. After a bit of meandering, I found the campground—a nice one—and pitched the tent. I settled up with the host the next day and ended up staying for two nights, saving £10 each night over the cost of the guesthouse.*

*If I had not had the tent, I probably would have asked if I could stay in the corner of the reception room until daylight. Then I would have found a café in the morning to consider my options over a nice cup of tea.*

*Another near miss: I confidently walked up to the immigration officer in Dublin's airport and handed him my passport. I had never had any problems entering a country and was surprised when he started asking some hard questions. It soon became apparent that he might not let me into the country. As I was stammering my answers, I began thinking about what I would do if that happened. I could not go back to the European continent—my EU Schengen Zone visa was expiring soon. I REALLY did not want to go home. The UK was close enough that a ticket would not cost so much, and I said to the officer, "Well, I guess I could get a ticket to England." For some reason, the officer seemed to back off a bit. However, as he stamped my passport, he said, "Don't make me sorry I did this."*

### The Lesson

In each of these cases, I immediately started thinking of solutions. Because my mind was occupied with solving the problem, I was less likely to panic.

Mental Health

## WHEN THINGS GO WRONG

I have been very fortunate during my years of traveling outside the US. I have only experienced minor mishaps—a few nasty falls (but no broken bones); a couple bad colds; and some near misses with travel plans. Although I am probably not the best advisor for what to do in a real disaster, here are two things that all experienced travelers advise:

- Have a travel insurance policy. Yes, I have written about this before, but it cannot be emphasized enough. The peace of mind I have experienced just from knowing that I could contact my insurance concierge service for any problems was worth the cost.
- If something happens, don't panic! Stop, take a few breaths. Look for allies and accept help.

Here are some other things you can do, depending on the urgency of solving the problem:

- Determine who can best be of assistance and put yourself in their hands. Medical personnel? Your embassy? The airline? Your travel insurance company? People nearby?
- Try to remain calm and reasonable. It is natural to want to find someone else to blame for your problems. Stay positive. I have found the magic words to say when asking for assistance are, "I am hoping you can help me." Most people really want to be helpful.
- Practice mindfulness. This will help you accept the circumstances and use the situation as a life lesson. See "Mindful Travel" in Chapter 12.
- Connect with friends and family members who care about you. They will look at your problem from a different perspective.
- Make a list of possible solutions. If you can, take plenty of time to make major decisions—preferably after a good rest.

*...Don't panic! Stop, take a few breaths. Look for allies and accept help.*

# Chapter Twelve

# Enhanced Travel

**In this Chapter...**

- Keep a Travel Journal
- Staying Creative
- Mindful Travel
- Thematic Travel

In this final chapter, I will explore some of the ways I have found to make my traveling days very special. Adding these layers to your travel dreams and plans will transform your journey from a list of destinations into an unforgettable adventure. I hope you can use these ideas to come up with ways to create your own unique travel style.

## Keep a Travel Journal

Even if you have never kept a journal before, consider trying it now. As you travel you will develop a journal style that works for you. I don't write every day, but mostly in fits and starts. I use my journal for a variety of things:

- A collection place for ephemera—tickets, receipts, brochures, coins, even my baggage claim tags!
- A problem solver. As mentioned in Chapter 11, I sometimes dump my problems over several pages and often come up with a solution.
- A list collector. I keep lists of blog post ideas, places I want to go, cool things I have experienced, and more.
- Expense tracker. As mentioned in Chapter 4, I jot down every penny I spend in my journal.
- A contacts collector. When I meet someone that I might want to contact later, I enter their email or other contact information in a special section in the back of the book.
- A place for daydreams and anticipations.

*A day in Sri Lanka. Two friends wrote my name in Tamil and Sinhalese script. I received my first "visiting" cards from a Hikkaduwa print shop. Also: currency samples expense records, and jottings for the day.*

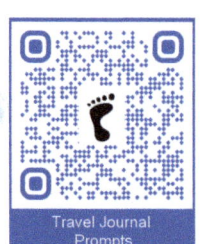

I am not very good at drawing or painting, so my pages are not nearly as beautiful as those you see when you search for travel journal ideas online. But when I look back over my journals, I realize that I would never trade them for something more artistic—they are MY journals.

There are many styles of travel journaling you can adopt. For more ideas, just google "travel journal ideas." To get you started, you can download a list of travel journaling prompts at CATHLEENSODYSSEY.COM/dpt-downloads

On the next page, I will introduce you to a very special method of journaling.

## STAYING CREATIVE

*Travel enhances creativity and creativity enhances travel.*

Don't leave your hobbies and pastimes at home. Make a list of the things you enjoy doing. Then start brainstorming the ways you might incorporate them into your travel plans. Here are a few things I worked on during my two-year sojourn:

- Cooking with local ingredients
- Photography and photo editing
- Video creation
- Writing and telling stories

*Enhanced Travel*

*A few of the hats I designed and knitted while in Scotland and Ireland from yarn I acquired there.*

- Knitting and spinning
- And then there was Hamish, The Traveling Scarf. (More about Hamish at the end of this chapter.)

As I mentioned in "Preventing Burnout" in Chapter 11, staying creative will not only enhance your travel experience, but it will help prevent travel burnout.

## MINDFUL TRAVEL

> *"Be alert to your own inner life while on the road and at the same time, appreciate the dignity and wonder all you encounter."*
> —*Jim Currie*

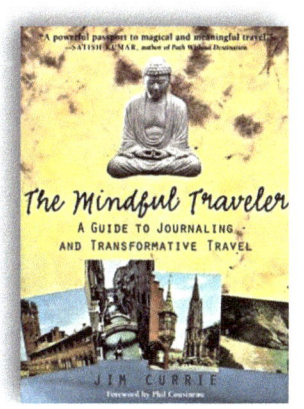

Before I traveled to Peru for the first time in 2014, I discovered a treasure of a book, *The Mindful Traveler*, by Jim Currie. It is now out of print, but you can probably find it in online stores that carry used books. *The Mindful Traveler* is a guide to using travel journals in a special way to be more respectful and aware and "enjoy each step that you take." Before you leave home, you establish "intentions," "touchstones," and "mandalas" (or mindsets), as well as ways to keep tabs on your well-being. Then you journal each day, so that you take time for reflection. By evaluating each day in terms of your health, intentions, and expectations, you become a more experienced and vital traveler.

Dream. Plan. Travel.

## HOW I USED *THE MINDFUL TRAVELER*

A favorite mandala that I created for myself was "Enlightened Warrior." Being aware of all my experiences—even the difficult or scary ones—helped me build my journeying skills.

Two intentions I set for myself were to relay my experiences to my friends and to learn new skills. My friends had made me promise to blog about my trip, but I had never written a blog before. I found that, in a different way from journaling, blogging made me creatively review my experiences and it forced me to digest them and present them in a way that would entertain others. The Cathleen's Odyssey blog has now become an important facet of all my travels.

One of my touchstones was to stay open to possibilities. One Sunday in Arequipa, Peru, I was planning to stay in and relax, work on my blog, and do some knitting. Adela, my host, knew that I was interested in the Festival of Candelaria that was going on in Puno and to which I was planning to travel in a few days. She came into my room and told me that she just heard on the radio that there would be a Candelaria procession in Arequipa starting that morning at one of the churches. I dropped everything, grabbed my camera and rushed out. I got to see one of the most colorful and festive parades of my life. Later I wrote in my journal:

> *As I approached the church, I saw people crowded around the door looking in. In the nearby park, dancers and bands were congregating, bands were warming up, and people in exotic costumes kept emerging from taxis. As I sat waiting, colorful fabrics surrounded me. Once the procession began—with firecrackers and bands playing and the Virgin emerging from the church—I was overwhelmed with all the commotion...*

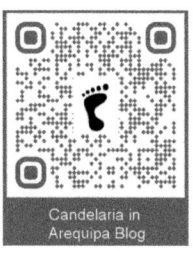
Candelaria in Arequipa Blog

You can read about and see what I would have missed if I had not stayed open to a change in my plans at:
CATHLEENSODYSSEY.COM/candelaria-1

A few other intentions, objectives, and touchstones I embraced while traveling included:
- Watch for coincidences and synchronicities
- Deny the seduction of self-guilt
- Reach out to strangers
- Don't let self-consciousness keep me from taking advantage of opportunities. (I am still working on this one!)

## Enhanced Travel

*A few of the "Mindful Travel" pages I created as I was planning how I would use this journaling method on my first trip to Peru in 2014.*

Mindful traveling led me to experience many "pinch myself" moments—those unexpected, euphoric episodes when, suddenly, you cannot believe what is happening. It is like you are the star in your own wonderful movie. You can read my blog about pinch-myself moments at **CathleensOdyssey.com/pinch-myself**

"Pinch-Myself Moments" Blog

Another proponent of mindful travel is Diana Winston, of UCLA's Mindful Awareness Research Center. She says that a mindful traveler is someone "who's respectful of the culture, who's not trying to impose their own culture, and who's willing to view the experience through a beginner's eyes rather than coming into it with expectations."

## THEMATIC TRAVEL

What do you enjoy doing? Fishing? Woodworking? Sewing? Painting? Gardening? Birdwatching? Gaming?

One method you can use to seek out kindred spirits is to travel thematically. Choose one or two things you enjoy and look for people who share your interest.

For example:
- Search out walking group events
- Have coffee and embroider with a new friend
- Talk shop with a fellow photographer

Dream. Plan. Travel.

- Find fellow chess players
- Help out in a neighborhood garden
- Learn how to cook regional specialties with locals
- Find other artists to sketch or paint with
- Attend star parties around the world
- Go open-water swimming with other enthusiasts

You can also look for themed museums and other attractions.

If you are reticent or shy, thematic travel is a great tool to break the ice, both for people you meet and for yourself. I now have friends all over the world, thanks to the way that I travel.

Ultimate Guide to Thematic Travel

*You can learn all about how to plan your own thematic journey in my online handbook "The Ultimate Guide to Thematic Travel." It includes a downloadable five-page Thematic Travel Planning Worksheet.*

**CATHLEENSODYSSEY.COM/thematic-travel**

"Coconut Sambol" Blog

*My daughter follows her cooking passion whenever she travels by shopping in traditional markets and then bringing the fresh ingredients back to her guesthouse to prepare fabulous meals. You can read an account and see a video of Rebecca shopping in the local market and then making Coconut Sambol in Malaysia at* **CATHLEENSODYSSEY.COM/coconut-sambol**

Enhanced Travel

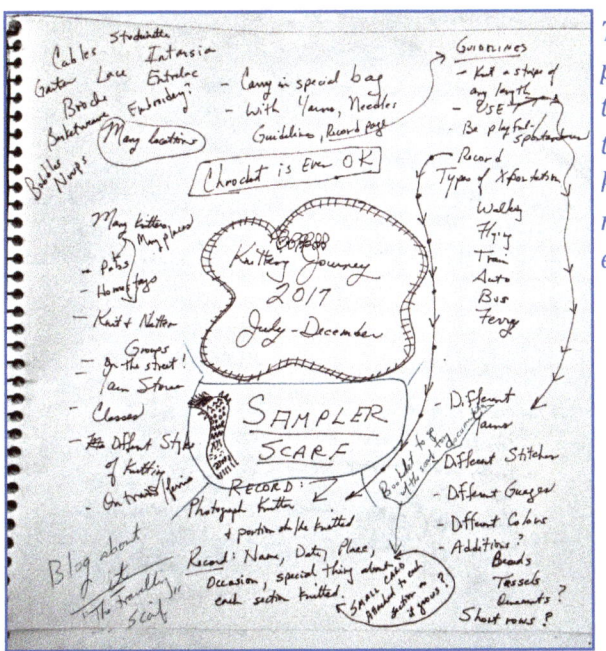

*This is one of the brainstorming pages I created as I planned a thematic participatory project to incorporate my passion for knitting into my journey. Read more about that project at the end of this chapter.*

**A Thematic Travel Project**

With a little thought, you can design a travel project for your theme that will link all the places you travel and people you meet. At the end of your trip, you will have a memento that will always remind you of your very special trip. Some examples are:
- Create a website about the project with photos and videos, along with simple captions.
- Create a journal detailing all the thematic events you attend. For example, if you are an amateur astronomer, make a new entry for each star party you attend. Include star charts, names and contact info for the people you meet, new things you learned, what you saw through those telescopes, etc.
- Author a blog based on your theme. Collect the emails of people you meet on your thematic journey and let them know when you publish a new blog post.
- Create a participatory project. For example, if you are an artist and planning to connect with other artists who draw or paint, carry a separate sketchpad just for inviting other artists to contribute their impressions. Keep a log for each contributor.

*Each contributor filled out a page in Hamish's journal. We reprinted the journal twice during the trip.*

*Hamish's youngest contributor was 13 years old, and the oldest was 90-year-old Linda Elgas, a well-known Estonian lace designer in Haapsalu, Estonia.*

# Hamish, the Traveling Scarf

Hamish was the participatory project I created for my knitting and spinning journey. Before my journey, I knitted a few rows of ribbing. As I traveled, I invited other knitters to add a few rows or a whole section—whatever they wanted…any stitch, any yarn, any pattern.

After a bit, the scarf developed a male persona, a somewhat snarky personality, and his own travel blog written from his point of view—even complaining when he wrote of being stuffed in his travel bag, or ignored while I went on walking holidays and left him behind. He also became quite an admirer of the ladies who handled him! Eventually, in Scotland, where we spent quite a bit of time, he acquired a very Scottish name, Hamish.

Hamish and I traveled to nine countries together. He had over 200 contributors and grew to six meters. He "wrote" 35 blog posts. I kept track of every contributor in special little journal books, and quite an assortment of knitters they were. The youngest was 13 years old and the oldest had passed 90. We found contributors in front of the Scottish Parliament on Women's Day, at the Roscommon Ireland Lamb Festival, at a Sheep Dog Trial, and we made a pilgrimage of sorts to the Knitted Lace Center in Haapsalu, Estonia. We saw the summer solstice in Iceland and knitted cozily in a tiny pub on Inish Mor while a 90-mile-an-hour January storm raged outside. We met knitters in the Outer Hebrides, funky hostels in Ireland, on English trains, and on ferries to remote islands. Some knitters added their own handspun yarn. We even occasionally allowed some crocheters to contribute—including a blind lady with her guide dog in Belfast.

At one point, as I was ghost-writing a post for Hamish–the one where he recounted how he got his name–he wrote, "Cathy decided that I had to have a very Scottish name: 'Hamish.' I love it…Hamish!…. It fits…Thank you, Cathy! I love you…"  And I burst into tears. I also had fallen in love with Hamish—and all the experiences we had together.

You can read Hamish's blog at
**CathleensOdyssey.com/traveling-scarf-blog**

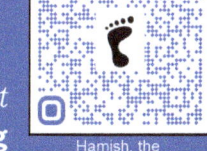

Hamish, the Traveling Scarf

# APPENDIX

**IN THIS CHAPTER...**

- Handbooks and How-Tos
- Favorite Places
- Favorite Blog Posts
- Cathleen's Odyssey Bookstore

## HANDBOOKS AND HOW-TOS ON MY WEBSITE

### The Ultimate Guide to Thematic Travel
CathleensOdyssey.com/thematic-travel

### Long Flight Survival Guide
CathleensOdyssey.com/long-flight-survival-guide

### Food Strategies for Affordable European Travel
CathleensOdyssey.com/FoodStrategies1
and
CathleensOdyssey.com/FoodStrategies2

### Dealing with Airport Taxi Paparazzi and Strategies for Market Shopping
CathleensOdyssey.com/taxi-paparazzi

### Turning Drudgery into an Adventure
CathleensOdyssey.com/drudgery-adventure

### Trip Planning Technique
CathleensOdyssey.com/planning-Spain-Netherlands

## FAVORITE PLACES

### Favorite Guest Houses and Hostels
Some of the links below may change over time. If you get "page not found" error, try searching in the booking engine with the name of the lodging.

**Peru**
Adela and Manuel's Guesthouse, Arequipa, Peru
www.airbnb.com/rooms/1510510?s=51

Casa Wilkamayo, Calca
www.airbnb.com/rooms/5457421?s=51

◀ *A lonely beach in winter.*     *Berneray Island, Outer Hebrides, Scotland.*

### Ecuador
Aylluwasi in Otavalo, Ecuador
CathleensOdyssey.com/aylluwasi

### UK & Ireland
Howmore Hostel, South Uist, Outer Hebrides, Scotland
www.gatliff.org.uk/howmore-hostel/

Elspeth's AirBnB Room, Glasgow, Scotland
www.airbnb.com/rooms/19145112?s=51

Black Sheep Hostel, Killarney, Ireland
CathleensOdyssey.com/black-sheep

Book the following through Hosteling International: **www.hihostels.com**

Islesburgh House Hostel, Lerwick, Shetland Islands, Scotland

Oban Hostel, Oban, Scotland

Rowan Tree Hostel, Ennis, Co Clare, Ireland

Book the following through YHA: **www.yha.org.uk**

Berwick-on-Tweed Hostel, England

YHA Hawes, Hawes, Yorkshire, England

### Estonia
Lõuna Hostel, Parnu, Estonia
CathleensOdyssey.com/hostel-louna

### Kyrgyzstan
Happy Nomads Yurt Camp
CathleensOdyssey.com/happy-nomads

Kurak Homestay, Bishkek, Kyrgyzstan
CathleensOdyssey.com/kurak

### Sri Lanka
Citadel Guesthouse, Hikkaduwa, Sri Lanka
CathleensOdyssey.com/the-citadel

Riviera Resort, Batticaloa, Sri Lanka
CathleensOdyssey.com/riviera-resort

### Malaysia
G Beach Front Villa, Tenjung Bungah, Penang, Malaysia
CathleensOdyssey.com/G-beach

### Favorite albergues on the Camino de Santiago del Norte and Primitivo
Albergue Piedad in Boo de Piélagos

Albergue Llanes Playa de Poo (This is not actually in the town of Llanes; it is in the village of Poo west of Llanes.)

Albergue de Perigrinos Villa de Grado—great breakfast!

Albergue de Perigrinos Bodenaya (on the Primitivo)

Casa Pepa Albergue in Santa Marina, La Coruña

Bella Muxia in Muxia on the Atlantic coast

# Appendix

## Bundle Up! My Favorite Winter Destinations
(Yes, it is cold, but read Chapter 9.)
- Inish Mor, Aran Islands, Ireland
- Outer Hebrides, Scotland
- Oban, Scotland
- Berwick on Tweed, England
- Alijo, Portugal

## My Favorite Walks/Hikes
- Almost any hike on the Isle of Arran, Scotland
- Any walk in the Outer Hebrides, Scotland
- Huchy Qusco Ruins, Sacred Valley, Peru
- Choquequirao (sister city to Machu Picchu), near Cachora, Peru
- Salinaras (Salt Farms) in Sacred Valley, near Urubamba, Peru
- Chinchero Valley, Near Urubamba, Peru
- Offa's Dyke, Wales
- Canal walking in the UK
- Douro Valley, near Alijo, Portugal
- The trails around Pitlochry, Scotland
- All around the beach of Gili Air, Lombok, Indonesia

## My Favorite Off-the-Beaten-Track Places
- Calca, Peru
- Outer Hebrides, Scotland
- Karokol and Jrygalan, Kyrgyzstan
- Santona, Spain
- Muxia, Spain
- Alijo, Portugal
- Shetland Islands, Scotland

# FAVORITE BLOG POSTS

## Favorite Food Posts

**Shopping...Cooking...Eating: Tamales! En Peru!**
CathleensOdyssey.com/tamales

**Shopping...Cooking...Eating: Chapter 1 Causa**
CathleensOdyssey.com/causa

**We Travel to Cook: Coconut Sambol**
CathleensOdyssey.com/coconut-sambol

Dream. Plan. Travel.

### Favorite Camino Blog

**Camino de Santiago del Norte – Day 11**
CathleensOdyssey.com/camino-day11

### Favorite Fiber Blog

**Picky about my Hentilagets on Bressay**
CathleensOdyssey.com/hentilagets

### Favorite "Confessions" Blog

I hope this one will help others for whom fear is a block to achieving their dreams.

**A Ship in the Harbor is Safe**
CathleensOdyssey.com/ship-in-the-harbor

### Favorite How-to Article

**Thematic Travel Handbook**
CathleensOdyssey.com/thematic-travel

### Favorite Local Encounter

**Nuevos Soles for New Soles**
CathleensOdyssey.com/soles-for-soles

### My Favorite Humorous Story

**How to Get Your Hair Washed, and NOT go to the Movies in Peru**
CathleensOdyssey.com/hair-wash

### Favorite Hiking (non-Camino) Blogs

**Growing Salt: The Salineras**
CathleensOdyssey.com/growing-salt

**Chinchero to Urquillos: All downhill...**
CathleensOdyssey.com/chinchero-hike

### Favorite Photographic Essays

**Trueno Y Relámpago! Tiempo Real!***
CathleensOdyssey.com/lightning

**Under the Douro Fog**
CathleensOdyssey.com/dourofog

### Favorite Introspective Blog

**The Art of Quitting: Finding Gratitude in Disappointment**
CathleensOdyssey.com/gratitude-1

### A Blog Post that Gives Me Hope

**Jyrgalan...The Phoenix of Kyrgyzstan**
CathleensOdyssey.com/jyrgalan-1

# Appendix

*Be sure to visit*
*Cathleen's Odyssey Bookstore*
*for more travelogues and how-to-travel books.*

### Food Strategies for Frugal Travelers
Cathy outlines easy ways to prepare healthy meals from fresh ingredients without spending a lot of time in the kitchen and without having to carry a lot of food in your pack. Enjoy whole-meal salads, fiber-filled breakfasts, and easy-to-make lunches for traveling days. Be prepared to cook under most any circumstance—even without a kitchen! Take advantage of all those bounteous European farmers markets to collect your ingredients. And you won't be giving up the opportunities to savor local specialties every once in a while.

### An Image Summons a Thousand Words
From the perspective of her twenty-first month as a solo independent traveler, Cathy shares a few favorite photographs from her odyssey along with the stories behind them—some touching, some funny, some to make you think, and all to inspire you to follow your own dreams—whether you are a traveler or not.

Use coupon code **DreamPlanTravel**
to receive 30% off at checkout.

## Acknowledgements

When you undertake a lengthy journey—especially a solo journey—you quickly discover that it is not something you really do alone. You need help in the form of advice and lots of backup while you are on the road.

This can take the form of being a "personal assistant back home" as my friends, Emily and Gar MacRae, and my ex-husband, Roger Fulton are. Emily and Gar let me store a whole bunch of stuff in their little home. And then they graciously accepted three large boxes of items I posted to them. Emily is always ready with advice when I cannot figure out what to do next and she is certainly the leader of my cheering squad. Roger has provided hundreds of hours of computer tech advice via Skype—he has helped me purchase and set up three (THREE!) laptops since I began traveling in 2014. One of them was an emergency purchase that I had make in Peru—and then we had to teach it to speak English! Everyone needs their own personal "techno-geek" and Roger is mine. (It is sure nice when your ex-husband is one of your best friends!)

My son Benjamin also helped with "techno-geek" experience. Before I embarked he helped me set up all the security systems on my computer.

Right in the middle of my journey, as I arrived in Kyrgyzstan, I received this email from Emily:

> *Would you like us to establish a GoFundMe campaign to get you an upgrade so moviemaking is easier and more fun? Jude gets credit for coming up with the idea...*

As a result, CathleensOdyssey.com was born. We created a crowdfunding campaign that provided a much-needed computer, camera, and software upgrade to make Cathleen's Odyssey possible. I doubt I would have ever tackled that job without the encouragement of Jude Spaith and Emily. So many thanks go to the donors who made the new equipment possible: Debbie Z., Sherry M., Hedy A., Margaret H., Barbara G., Caitlin B., Jude S., Karen B., Amy M., Merrilee R., Beth T., Annie S., Karen D., Rebecca J., Emily and Gar M., Nan W., Myra W., Vashon Fibershed, Janice B., and Joe and Zule M.

As I wrote about in this book, you need a cheering squad, and mine spanned the world as I gathered up new friends along the way. I know I am going to leave someone out, but here goes (in no particular order): Herdis in Iceland; Debbie, Anne, Catherine, Marie, Catherine in Scotland;

Annie, Nev, and Peter in England; Arlette, Marie, and Laura in Portugal; Caitlin and Gerry, Phil, Noel, Bridgid, Deborah in Ireland; Connie and Gerard, Nas and Frederick, Janneke, Lili, and Jantine in the Netherlands; Charlotte in Finland; Jared in Sweden; Astrit in Estonia; Tulasi in India; Karen in Oman; Tynch, Altynai, Saltanat, and Bakytbek in Kyrgyzstan; Tedi in Indonesia; Raj and Elma in Sri Lanka; Roee in Israel; Adela and Manuel in Peru; Gülçiçek and Grace in Malaysia; Marcie and Charlie, Zule and Jose, Elmer and Colleen, Rosanne and Rodney, Jeff, Deborah, Steffon, Bob and Margot, Gail, Judy, Gail, Nan, Sue, Lyle and Lily, Heidi, Ann, Mary, Carla, LaHuan, Don and Gayle, Michelle, Rebecca, Mark, Diane, Myra, Rosa, Sherri, Jillian, Joe, Amy, Kate, Karen, Linda, Amy, Starla, Merrilee, Felicia, Karen, Gloria, Barbara, Tom, Candy, Jude, Sheila, Veryl, May and John, Hedy, Maggie, Jeanne, Jeff, Jonna, Veryl, Michael and Diane, Sandy, Patrick, Miquela, cousins Billy, Butch, Sherley, Pam, Pat, Charlotte, and Bob, sister Janice, and, of course, my son Benjamin in the US.

A great big thanks goes out to my Facebook friends who critiqued and made suggestions for various parts of this book.

Manuel and Adela in Arequipa, Peru put up with me every day for over a month while I took over their dining table to put the finishing touches on the book.

My sister, Janice Bailey is one of my head cheerleaders. She follows my every move around the globe, making sure I am safe and that I am reporting my status regularly. I really needed a proofreader and without my asking her, she proofed this entire book as a gift. When I returned home, she helped me organize my first travel presentation so I can continue my travel education pursuits in the United States. Everyone should have a sister like Janice!

And then there is my daughter Rebecca. She provided myriad suggestions for improving the quality of this book over the months I worked on it. Not only that, I could not have survived the trip without her hours of talk, encouragement, commiseration, advice, and giggles on the phone. She joined me TWICE along the way (in Portugal and Malaysia), and we look forward to our joint odyssey in 2020.

And to all the people who asked me questions about my trip and how I travel. It is you for whom I wrote this book.

## About the Author

Cathy Fulton has been a world nomad since 2014. She is a citizen of the United States, but she does not have a permanent residence. Cathy considers herself as a solo, independent, slow, long-term, and frugal traveler. This means that she plans and books all her own travel and does not go on organized tours. Her goal is to travel cheaply so that it is financially sustainable. Hostel dorm rooms and small guest houses are usually her temporary homes.

Cathy looks for ways to experience cultures deeply as she travels. She has found the best way to engage with locals is by using a technique called "thematic travel." She looks for people around the world who share her passion for food and the fiber arts, and she uses these common interests to break the ice. As a result, she has met hundreds of people, many of whom have become lifelong friends.

What started as a mere six-month trip to Europe in 2017, expanded to a two-year odyssey spanning 17 countries around the world. When asked what her address is, she is hard-pressed to give you an answer.

Cathy loves to share her stories and traveling methods to encourage others to step outside their self-imposed boundaries and follow their travel dreams.

You can learn more about Cathy's way of life on her website and blog, CATHLEENSODYSSEY.COM, where you will find stories, how-to guides, and inspiration. As Cathy likes to remind everyone,

*Life begins outside your comfort zone!*

www.ingramcontent.com/pod-product-compliance
Lightning Source LLC
Chambersburg PA
CBHW040732020526
44112CB00059B/2950